WINKING AT DESTINY

A JOURNEY INTO CONSCIOUSNESS

BY

SHARON PACIONE

LIBRARY OF CONGRESS CATALOG CARD NUMBER: 97-93837

ISBN 0-9658394-0-0

BOOK FORMATTED BY DARLENE MUDRICK (OSAGE, WV); TYPESET IN 9 POINT CANCUN

PRINTED AND BOUND BY BOOKMASTERS, INC., MANSFIELD, OHIO

PUBLISHER

BOX 360421
STRONGSVILLE, OHIO 44136

FIRST EDITION
FIRST PRINTING JANUARY 1998
RECYCLED PAPER

SO TAKE MY HAND
AND LET US WALK
TOGETHER

WITH A STUMBLE
AND A CRY
ALONG THE WAY

BUT LAUGHTER, TOO
AND LOVE

AND KNOWLEDGE
THAT AS IT IS FOR ME
SO IT WILL BE FOR YOU.

JOHN PATRICK DAVIS
FROM THE BOOK "CHRYSALIS"

I WANT THE WORLD TO KNOW THAT WITHOUT THE
"BEYOND THE CALL OF DUTY" EFFORT OF DARLENE
MUDRICK, THIS BOOK WOULD HAVE HAD TO WAIT
ANOTHER LIFETIME TO BE PUBLISHED. THANK YOU,
FRIEND.

THANK YOU JACQUI, LINDA, AND LINDA FOR YOUR
HELP DURING THE "LABOR PAINS" STAGE OF THE
BOOK.

DEDICATIONS

TO THE CREATOR FOR LIGHTING MY PATH WITH MAGNIFICENT TEACHERS IN MANY DIMENSIONS OF REALITY. I AM ESPECIALLY GRATEFUL FOR THE GIFTS OF PATIENCE AND UNDERSTANDING DURING THE TIMES THAT I DIDN'T INITIALLY REALIZE HOW "MAGNIFICENT" SOME OF THESE TEACHERS WERE. THE ROAD WAS SOMETIMES BUMPY, BUT THE LIGHTS WERE ALWAYS WHITE.

LOVE IS THE ULTIMATE CREATIVE FORCE IN THE UNIVERSE. LOVE IS STRENGTH, NOT WEAKNESS OR VULNERABILITY. REMEMBER THAT THE MASTER CHRIST TAUGHT LOVE AS A SOLUTION TO ALL THINGS. BUT ALSO REMEMBER THAT YOU HAVE THE FREE WILL TO SAY "NO" TO ESTABLISHED SOCIAL AND RELIGIOUS INSTITUTIONS THAT TEACH FEAR AND INTOLERANCE.

- RICHARD DANNELLEY
SEDONA: BEYOND THE VORTEX

TO MY HUSBAND, JERRY, AND OUR CHILDREN ANDREA AND NICK FOR THEIR UNCONDITIONAL LOVE AND SUPPORT OF MY QUEST FOR KNOWLEDGE AND UNDERSTANDING OF THE MYSTERIES OF LIFE, AND TO ALL OF MY FAMILY AND FRIENDS FOR THEIR GIFTS OF HUMOR AND TRUST DURING THE TIMES THAT NONE OF US KNEW WHERE THIS JOURNEY WOULD LEAD; ESPECIALLY TO MY SISTER MERILYNN FOR HER LOVE AND SENSE OF ADVENTURE ON THIS JOURNEY INTO CONSCIOUSNESS.

GRATITUDE SMILES ON THE ANCIENT ONES IN ALL RACES AND CULTURES FOR HAVING THE COURAGE TO LIVE THE MYSTERY, AND FOR LEAVING US A TREASURE CHEST OF CLUES FOR THE EVOLUTION OF OUR COLLECTIVE SOUL.

TO THE LIGHTWORKERS ON AND OFF THE PLANET, MAY YOUR ACCELERATED JOURNEY OF WONDER CONTINUE TO BE BLESSED.

AS WE MOVE FROM THE UNCARING, ILLUSIONARY WORLD THAT MANY CALL REALITY, PERHAPS ONE DAY SOON WE WILL PROGRESS FROM A PLACE OF DENIAL ABOUT WHO WE HAVE BECOME AS A HUMAN SPECIES INTO BEINGS OF UNCONDITIONAL LOVE AND ACCEPTANCE OF ALL LIFEFORMS IN ALL REALITIES. HEAVEN KNOWS, THE CREATOR HAS GIVEN US ENOUGH CHOICES.

IF IN THE TWILIGHT OF MEMORY WE SHOULD MEET ONCE MORE, WE SHALL SPEAK AGAIN TOGETHER AND YOU SHALL SING TO ME A DEEPER SONG. AND IF OUR HANDS SHOULD MEET IN ANOTHER DREAM WE SHALL BUILD ANOTHER TOWER IN THE SKY.
                                    - KAHLIL GIBRAN
                                      THE PROPHET

TO MY NIECES MARY ELLEN AND SHERI AND THE OTHER WOMEN OF *CIRCLE OF STONES*, "OM NAMAHA SHIVAYA".

THANK YOU CHRIS K. FOR INITIALLY TYPING THIS BOOK AND FOR YOUR MUCH APPRECIATED ENCOURAGEMENT.

CIRCLE OF STONES

DEE ALLMAN	ALMA SNIDER
LYNN BOERTJE	ROSE WELCHANS
CHRIS KRZEMINSKI	MARY ELLEN WOJIE
SHERI LUCIUS	LIZ YANOK
MARIE PIZZO	DEE ZUCHETTO

TO THE MANY ASPECTS OF MYSELF THAT I MEET EVERYDAY IN OTHERS, I AM GRATEFUL FOR THE REFLECTIONS. I ACCEPT ALL LESSONS AS BLESSINGS IN HELPING ME TO BECOME AWARE OF MY POTENTIAL, AND I APPRECIATE THE OPPORTUNITY TO SHARE THE JOURNEY WITH YOU.

> *THE REAL MYSTERY OF LIFE IS NOT A PROBLEM TO BE SOLVED. IT IS A REALITY TO BE EXPERIENCED.*
> *- J. J. VAN DER LEEUW*

MANY ANIMAL KINGDOM TEACHERS OF LAND, AIR AND WATER HOLD A SPECIAL PLACE OF HONOR IN MY HEART FOR THEIR PRESENCE/PRESENTS IN MY LIFE. FROM THEM I HAVE LEARNED ABOUT UNCONDITIONAL LOVE, STRENGTH, GRACE, FAMILY, COOPERATION, WORK ETHIC, PATIENCE, FEAR, DEVOTION, SPONTANEITY, POWER, INDEPENDENCE, PLAYFULNESS, PERSEVERANCE, FREEDOM, INTUITION, RHYTHM, CLEANLINESS, THE VALUE OF GOING WITHIN, BLENDING IN, TRUST, EXPECTING THE UNEXPECTED, LOOKING BEYOND THE HORIZON, LOYALTY, GENTLENESS, CREATIVITY, LIVING IN MULTIPLE REALMS, BEAUTY, NOT TO BE THIN SKINNED, THE POWER OF SILENCE/STILLNESS, ENJOYING THE NECTAR OF LIFE, THE IMPORTANCE OF TRANSFORMATION, COMMUNITY, FRIENDSHIP, PROTECTION, SURVIVAL, NAVIGATING IN THE DARK, REFLECTING THE LIGHT, GIANT LEAPS FORWARD, PAYING ATTENTION TO THE DREAMTIME, CONNECTING TO MOTHER EARTH, SENSITIVITY TO VIBRATIONS, LIVING THE MYSTERY AND, MOST OF ALL, THAT EVERYTHING AND EVERYBODY HAS A PURPOSE. EVERYTHING AND EVERYONE IS OUR TEACHER, AND THAT ALL PATHS ARE SACRED.

IF YOU TALK TO THE ANIMALS THEY WILL TALK WITH YOU AND YOU WILL KNOW EACH OTHER. IF YOU DO NOT TALK TO THEM, YOU WILL NOT KNOW THEM, AND WHAT YOU DO NOT KNOW YOU WILL FEAR. WHAT ONE FEARS, ONE DESTROYS.
                                        - CHIEF DAN GEORGE

TO THE PLANT AND MINERAL KINGDOMS, THANK YOU FOR SUCH INCREDIBLE GIFTS OF BEAUTY AND FOR PROVIDING EVERYTHING NECESSARY FOR US TO HEAL OURSELVES NATURALLY. MAYBE WHEN WE STOP TRYING TO RE-INVENT THE WHEEL, WE'LL SEE WHAT HAS BEEN HERE ALL ALONG.

WE ARE BLESSED TO LIVE ON A PLANET OF SUCH BEAUTY AND DIVERSITY. MAY THE SUN CONTINUE TO RISE AND SET EVERY DAY IN OUR SPECK OF THE UNIVERSE AS WE COME TO OUR SENSES AND REALIZE HOW FORTUNATE WE ARE.

WHERE PLANTS HAVE FIVE-FOLD PATTERNS, A CONSIDERATION OF THEIR SOULS IS IN PLACE. FOR PATTERNS OF FIVE APPEAR IN THE REGULAR SOLIDS, AND SO INVOLVE THE RATIO CALLED THE GOLDEN SECTION, WHICH RESULTS FROM A SELF-DEVELOPING SERIES THAT IS AN IMAGE OF THE FACULTY OF PROPAGATION IN PLANTS. THUS THE FLOWER CARRIES THE AUTHENTIC FLAG OF THIS FACULTY, THE PENTAGON.

- JOHANNES KEPLER

A SPECIAL THANK YOU TO TWO OF THE KINDEST,
WISEST TEACHERS ON THE PLANET.

TED ANDREWS

&

RAINBOW EAGLE

POEMS

SYMBOLS

WOLVES BREED IN CAPTIVITY, BUT IT SEEMS UNLIKELY THAT A WOLF WHO IS CONSTANTLY BEING STARED AT FROM NEARBY, A WOLF WITH NO PLACE TO HIDE, A WOLF WHO CANNOT SEE THE MOON, CAN BE A CONTENTED WOLF.

— WHEN ELEPHANTS WEEP

ANIMALS ALSO TRY TO RESCUE THEIR YOUNG FROM DANGERS OTHER THAN PREDATORS . . . EXPLORER PETER FREUCHEN CAME ACROSS A FAMILY OF SIX WOLVES, TWO ADULTS AND FOUR CUBS. THE WOLVES WERE HOWLING. ONE OF THE CUBS WAS CAUGHT IN A TRAP SET AT A CAIRN OF STONES OVER A FOOD CACHE. THE OTHER WOLVES HAD OVERTURNED MANY OF THE LARGE STONES AND SCRAPED THE FROZEN EARTH AROUND THE STONE TO WHICH THE TRAP WAS FASTENED IN THEIR EFFORTS TO FREE THE CUB. WHEN HUMANS PROTECT THEIR YOUNG THIS WAY WE CALL IT LOVE.

- WHEN ELEPHANTS WEEP

WOULDST READ THE STORY OF THE SELF-BORN KING?
FIRST LEARN THE SPLENDID LANGUAGE OF THE SUN,
THE SPEECH OF THE STARS, THE MOON'S COY
WHISPERING, THE MUSIC OF THE PLANETS, AND OF
ONE, OUR MOTHER EARTH, CROONING HER CRADLE-
SONG TO HER UNCOUNTED BABES, WHO, WHEN THEY
GAIN THE SOUL'S FULL STATURE, TO THE HEAVENS
BELONG. . .

— JAMES MORGAN PRYSE

THERE IS A PLANET

WHERE ILLUSION IS THE ACCEPTED REALITY

WHERE EGO IS KING

WHERE WAR MONGERS FLEX THEIR NUCLEAR MUSCLES,
CREATING WARS TO BOOST THE ECONOMY,
KEEPING THE MASSES BOUND TO FALSE HOPE
THAT THEY LIVE ON A SAFE PLANET

WHERE FORGOTTEN PRISONERS OF LONG-AGO WARS
LIVE THE HORRIBLE TRUTH OF ABANDONMENT

WHERE LESS THAN 2% OF THE POPULATION
DETERMINES THE ECONOMIC STRUCTURE
FOR THE OTHER 98%

WHERE GOVERNMENT REPRESENTATIVES
ARE BOUGHT AND PAID FOR
BY LOBBYISTS WITH PRIVATE INTERESTS,
AND WHERE DECISIONS ARE NOT
BASED ON WHAT IS FOR THE GOOD OF ALL

WHERE INDIVIDUALS ACCUMULATE MORE WEALTH
THAN THEY CAN POSSIBLY USE,
HOARDING RATHER THAN SHARING
WITH THOSE LESS FORTUNATE,
BECAUSE OF FEAR OF LOSING THEIR POSITION
ON A MEDIA CREATED LIST
OF "WEALTHIEST PEOPLE IN THE WORLD"...
SOMETIMES, FOR AN EVEN SADDER REASON,
BECAUSE THEY DON'T CARE

WHERE THE OZONE LAYER HAS DIMINISHED,
CAUSING GLOBAL WARMING,
REDUCING AN ALREADY SHRINKING LAND MASS
HOUSING 5.5 BILLION PEOPLE
AND COUNTLESS OTHER LIFEFORMS

WHERE CHILDREN ARE ABUSED
AND OFTEN DIE
AT THE HANDS OF THOSE TRUSTED
TO PROTECT THEM

WHERE THE EYES OF STARVATION
AND HOMELESSNESS STARE BLANKLY
INTO THOSE OF ACCEPTANCE

WHERE HATRED RULES
RACIAL AND RELIGIOUS INTOLERANCE
AS AN ACCEPTED FORM
OF FREEDOM OF EXPRESSION

WHERE THERE IS NO REVERENCE FOR WISDOM
THAT COMES WITH EXPERIENCE AND AGE

WHERE DESTRUCTION OF THE INTERIOR
AND EXTERIOR OF THE PLANET
IS LOOKED UPON WITH APATHY

WHERE POLLUTION RAINS
AND WATER IS SO CONTAMINATED
THAT FISH COMMIT SUICIDE

WHERE FREE ENERGY FOR ALL
IS NOT UNVEILED
BECAUSE INDUSTRY CAN OUTRAGEOUSLY
CONTINUE TO CHARGE FOR THE CURRENT SYSTEM

WHERE MAN CAN ROCKET TO THE MOON,
BUT CANNOT SOLVE THE PROBLEM OF OVER-POPULATION

WHERE DEAD SOIL GROWS DEAD FOOD

WHERE OTHER LIFEFORMS ARE CONSUMED AS FOOD

xx

WHERE THE MEDICAL SYSTEM
CONCENTRATES MORE ON TREATING ILLNESS
THAN PREVENTING IT,
BECAUSE THEY HAVE LOST THEIR CONNECTION TO NATURE

WHERE WITH EVERY GENERATION
A NEW DISEASE BECOMES PREVALENT
CAUSING CHRONIC DETERIORATION OF THE PHYSICAL BODY

WHERE NEWS MEDIA THRIVES ON BAD NEWS,
ON THE PROFITS OF MURDER AND WAR,
AND GOOD NEWS IS CONSIDERED BORING
AND NOT PROFITABLE

WHERE PRISON GUARDS AND OFFICIALS
TURN THEIR HEADS
TO THE RAPE OF YOUNG MEN AND WOMEN,
FINALLY CAUGHT BY AN ARM OF THE SAME SYSTEM
THAT IGNORED NEGLECT AND ABUSE
IN THE NOW ADULT'S FORMATIVE YEARS

WHERE BABY SEALS ARE CLUBBED TO DEATH
IN FRONT OF THEIR MOTHERS,
HUNTED FOR THEIR SOFT WHITE FUR

WHERE DEER HANG AS TROPHIES ON FAMILY ROOM WALLS,
STARING AT THEIR CAPTORS WITH EYES OF THE HUNTED

WHERE RHINOS ARE SLAUGHTERED FOR THEIR HORNS
SO THAT HUMANS CAN SATISFY SEXUAL CURIOSITY

WHERE ELEPHANTS ARE MASSACRED FOR THEIR TUSKS,
CARVED INTO FIGURES FOR LIVING ROOM TABLES

WHERE DOLPHINS BREATHE THEIR DYING BREATH
ENSNARED IN A NET,
GRASPING AT FREEDOM

WHERE POWER AND CONTROL
EAT FOR LUNCH
COMPASSION AND INTEGRITY

WHERE, TO OTHERS IN THE UNIVERSE,
THOSE ON THIS PLANET ARE ALIEN...
SICK IN BODY, MIND AND SPIRIT

WHERE IS THIS PLANET?
THIS PLANET IS EARTH!

IF THESE CONDITIONS
CONTINUE TO RING ON INDIFFERENT EARS,
THEN OUR MIND HAS INDEED
BECOME A RUG PILED HIGH WITH THE DEBRIS
THAT HAS BEEN SWEPT UNDER IT

WHEN A LARGE SEGMENT OF THE POPULATION
IS PROUD TO SAY "BUT, WE STILL LIVE
IN THE GREATEST COUNTRY IN THE WORLD"
IT IS PROOF THAT WE HAVE ANESTHETIZED OURSELVES
WITH OUR ADDICTIONS,
CHOOSING TO LIVE A COMFORTABLY NUMB LIFE,
INDIFFERENT TO THE SUFFERING OF ALL FORMS OF LIFE,
INCLUDING THE PLANET HERSELF

WE HAVE FAILED AS CARETAKERS.
THE TIME HAS COME
WHEN IT IS NO LONGER ACCEPTABLE
TO JEOPARDIZE THE BALANCE
OF OUR HOME AND THE UNIVERSE

THESE VOICES, AND THE SILENT SCREAMS
OF THE VOICES NOT HEARD,
ARE WHY THE COSMIC GUARDIANS
KNOWN AS "STAR PEOPLE"
ARE ONCE AGAIN MAKING THEMSELVES KNOWN.
THEY HAVE HEARD THE S.O.S. ECHOES OF OUR MOTHER

PLANET EARTH CAN RECOVER,
BUT WE MUST FIRST REALIZE THAT WE'RE ILL.
WE CAN ALL SERVE THE PROCESS
BY HEALING OUR OWN BODY, MIND AND SPIRIT,
BY CHOOSING LOVE OVER FEAR,
BY PICKING OUR PASSION AND GETTING INVOLVED.
WHICH MOMENT WILL YOU CHOOSE TO REMEMBER
THAT ONE PERSON CAN MAKE A DIFFERENCE?

PEACE AND LOVE MULTIPLY WHEN WE DIVIDE IT WITH
OTHERS.
- ST. JOSEPH CHURCH SIGNBOARD
STRONGSVILLE, OHIO

BUDDHIST GOTHA

IN THE GARBAGE I SEE A ROSE
IN THE ROSE, I SEE THE GARBAGE
EVERYTHING IS IN TRANSFORMATION
EVEN PERMANENCE IS IMPERMANENT

PEOPLES OF ELDER CULTURES
OFTEN SAY THAT THE SURVIVAL OF HUMAN BEINGS
DEPENDS ON BEING ABLE TO HEAR
THE LANGUAGE OF THE BIRDS AND BEASTS,
THE LANGUAGE OF THE RIVER, ROCK, AND WIND,
BEING ABLE TO UNDERSTAND WHAT IS BEING SAID
IN ALL TONGUES OF PLANT, CREATURE & ELEMENT.
LISTENING TO THE GARBAGE AS WELL AS THE ROSE,
WITH THE SAME EARS,
THE EARS OF COMPASSIONATE UNDERSTANDING.

JOAN HALIFAX
THE FRUITFUL DARKNESS:
RECONNECTING WITH THE BODY OF THE EARTH

BURIED TREASURE

TRUTH
DOES NOT SIT GLEAMING
ON A MOUNTAINTOP
WAITING
TO BE DISCOVERED

MORE OFTEN
IT'S FOUND BURIED
IN A PILE OF RUBBLE
PATIENTLY AWAITING
SEEKERS OF TREASURE

INVARIABLY
THE RUBBLE OF THE MIND
IS THE HEAVIEST

DON'T BE AFRAID
TO DIG IN

THE EARTH IS RUDE, SILENT, INCOMPREHENSIBLE AT FIRST. NATURE IS INCOMPREHENSIBLE AT FIRST. BE NOT DISCOURAGED, KEEP ON. THERE ARE DIVINE THINGS WELL ENVELOP'D, I SWEAR TO YOU THERE ARE DIVINE BEINGS MORE BEAUTIFUL THAN WORDS CAN TELL.

- WALT WHITMAN (1819-1892)
AMERICAN POET

EL MORYA

I WASN'T AWARE OF EL MORYA
WHEN OUT OF THE BLUE HE CAME
HIS WORDS CAME IN SILENCE
LIFE WOULD NEVER BE THE SAME

EL MORYA IS PART OF THE FIRST RAY
ARCHANGEL MICHAEL IS HIS BOSS
QUESTIONING WHY HE'D CONTACT ME
I WAS COMPLETELY AT A LOSS

THE MESSAGE WAS VERY SIMPLISTIC
TO HEAL MYSELF WAS THE THEME
FOR PART OF MY LIFE PURPOSE
IS TO BE AN EXAMPLE OF POTENTIAL IT SEEMS

WITHIN DAYS I STARTED WRITING
MY FEELINGS JUST SEEMED TO FLOW
THERE WAS LOVE, COMPASSION, WONDER AND TEARS
MY SOUL WAS SIMPLY AGLOW

THOUGH DISCERNMENT IS VERY IMPORTANT
DON'T LET FEAR OF THE UNKNOWN BIND
BENEVOLENCE FOLLOWS A LOVING HEART
SEEKING PLAYERS OF EVERY KIND

AWARENESS IS FORMED OF COURAGE
BY TRUSTING WHAT SLEEPS INSIDE
CONTACT WITH OTHER DIMENSIONS
AWAKENS WONDER THAT BLOWS THE MIND

BURIED TREASURE

TRUTH
DOES NOT SIT GLEAMING
ON A MOUNTAINTOP
WAITING
TO BE DISCOVERED

MORE OFTEN
IT'S FOUND BURIED
IN A PILE OF RUBBLE
PATIENTLY AWAITING
SEEKERS OF TREASURE

INVARIABLY
THE RUBBLE OF THE MIND
IS THE HEAVIEST

DON'T BE AFRAID
TO DIG IN

EL MORYA

I WASN'T AWARE OF EL MORYA
WHEN OUT OF THE BLUE HE CAME
HIS WORDS CAME IN SILENCE
LIFE WOULD NEVER BE THE SAME

EL MORYA IS PART OF THE FIRST RAY
ARCHANGEL MICHAEL IS HIS BOSS
QUESTIONING WHY HE'D CONTACT ME
I WAS COMPLETELY AT A LOSS

THE MESSAGE WAS VERY SIMPLISTIC
TO HEAL MYSELF WAS THE THEME
FOR PART OF MY LIFE PURPOSE
IS TO BE AN EXAMPLE OF POTENTIAL IT SEEMS

WITHIN DAYS I STARTED WRITING
MY FEELINGS JUST SEEMED TO FLOW
THERE WAS LOVE, COMPASSION, WONDER AND TEARS
MY SOUL WAS SIMPLY AGLOW

THOUGH DISCERNMENT IS VERY IMPORTANT
DON'T LET FEAR OF THE UNKNOWN BIND
BENEVOLENCE FOLLOWS A LOVING HEART
SEEKING PLAYERS OF EVERY KIND

AWARENESS IS FORMED OF COURAGE
BY TRUSTING WHAT SLEEPS INSIDE
CONTACT WITH OTHER DIMENSIONS
AWAKENS WONDER THAT BLOWS THE MIND

SURPRISE CAPTURES EACH MOMENT
AS I CONTEMPLATE EACH NEW DARE
THIS SYNCHRONISTIC SYMPHONY
PLAYS THE MUSIC OF LIFE WITH FLAIR

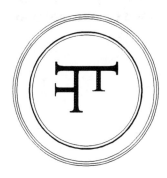

THE EYE WITH WHICH I PERCEIVE GOD IS THE SAME
EYE WITH WHICH GOD PERCEIVES ME.
- MEISTER ECKHART
14TH CENTURY

DEAFENING SILENCE

THERE'S A DIFFERENCE BETWEEN THE INTELLIGENT MIND
AND THE SIMPLE LOGIC OF MAN
AN EXAMPLE IS BUILDING A NUCLEAR PLANT
NEAR A FAULT LINE BECAUSE WE CAN

WHERE'S THE CARE AND CONCERN FOR LIFE
HAVE WE BURIED OUR HEADS IN THE SAND
TIME STILL REMAINS TO CORRECT THESE MISTAKES
EARTH IS ALL LIFEFORMS' LAND

TECHNOLOGY AT THE EXPENSE OF LIFE
IS NEVER THE RIGHT CHOICE
OUR SILENCE IS CLEARLY DEAFENING
WHILE WE CAN, LET'S RESPOND AS ONE VOICE

WHERE THERE IS NO VISION, PEOPLE PERISH.
- PROVERBS 29:18

WHAT COLOR IS LOVE

IN ANCHORING LOVE ON THE PLANET
WE TRAVEL TO SACRED SITES
SOME NATIVE BROTHERS DON'T KNOW US
THOUGH WE HONOR AN ANCIENT PLIGHT

WE'RE MANY SHADES THIS LIFETIME
AND OUR ENERGIES ARE WED
PLEASE LOOK A LITTLE CLOSER
IT'S OUR HEART NOT FACE THAT'S RED

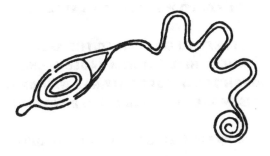

MEN ARE DISTURBED NOT BY THINGS THAT HAPPEN,
BUT BY THEIR OPINION OF THE THINGS THAT HAPPEN.

- EPICTETUS

THE FLAVOR OF COMPASSION

LEAVING HIS HOME UNDER A BRIDGE
A BEGGAR TOOK A WALK
WINDING THROUGH CROWDS OF PEOPLE
FOR A MOMENT OUR EYES WOULD LOCK

"WILL YOU BUY ME A HAMBURGER"
HE ASKED SOMEONE IN OUR GROUP
WE WERE ON OUR WAY TO A BALLGAME
NO TIME LEFT TO FEED HIM TOO

AT OUR TABLE WE HAD A DISCUSSION
ABOUT PEOPLE WHO BEG FOR FOOD
THE CONSENSUS WAS OVERWHELMING
HE COULD WORK IF HE WANTED TO

I LEFT TO GO BACK TO THE AREA
WHERE HE'D SAT AT A TABLE ALONE
THOUGH THE OPPORTUNITY HAD WITHDRAWN
HIS IMAGE REMAINED CARVED IN STONE

WE'RE PRESENTED OCCASIONAL POP QUIZZES
TO INVENTORY WHAT'S INSIDE
HOW LONG WILL IT TAKE TO REALIZE
THERE BUT FOR THE GRACE OF GOD GO I

THIS MAN WAS A POWERFUL TEACHER
IN A PURE AND SIMPLE FASHION
I RETURNED TO MY OWN MEAL TO FIND
IT LACKED THE DISTINCT FLAVOR OF COMPASSION

GOD CREATED THE UNIVERSE THROUGH THE BREATH
OF THE COMPASSIONATE.

- MOHAMMED
(C. 570-632)

SLEEP TIGHT

HOW CAN WE SLEEP AT NIGHT
WHEN OUR CHILDREN LIE AWAKE WITH FRIGHT
FROM BEING NEGLECTED AND SLAPPED AROUND
THEY STARE AT LIFE THROUGH A FROZEN FROWN

HOW CAN WE SLEEP AT NIGHT
WHILE HOMELESS SEEK SHELTER UNDER STREET LIGHTS
AND WALK BY DAY FROM PLACE TO PLACE
WITH THE PAIN OF LONELINESS ON THEIR FACE

HOW CAN WE SLEEP AT NIGHT
WHEN JUNKIES ROAM OUR STREETS AS HIGH AS KITES
TRYING TO SCORE DRUGS OF EVERY KIND
BECOMING PRISONERS OF THEIR MINDS

HOW CAN WE SLEEP AT NIGHT
AS CASUALTIES OF WAR DIE LEFT AND RIGHT
AND THE SCREAMS OF INNOCENT VICTIMS SOAR
TO JOIN OTHERS NEAR DEATH'S DOOR

HOW CAN WE SLEEP AT NIGHT
WHEN THERE'S STILL DISSENSION BETWEEN BLACK AND
WHITE
AND NO ONE WANTS TO ACCEPT THE BLAME
FOR THE MANY CENTURIES OF GUILT AND SHAME

HOW CAN WE SLEEP AT NIGHT
WHEN WE DON'T TRY WITH ALL OUR MIGHT
TO RIGHT THE WRONGS WE SEE EACH DAY
WE HAVE TO DO MORE THAN PRAY

HOW CAN WE IGNORE THE PAIN
AND LET DENIAL RULE OUR BRAIN
BY PRETENDING THAT OUR WORLD IS BRIGHT
IF IT'S ONLY A DREAM, *SLEEP TIGHT*

UNLESS WE CHANGE DIRECTION WE ARE LIKELY TO END
UP WHERE WE ARE HEADED.
                              - CHINESE PROVERB

KNOCK, KNOCK...IS ANYBODY HOME

IF WE ONLY USE 10% OF OUR BRAIN
WHAT CLAIMS THE REMAINING PERCENT
EITHER LEARN TO UNLOCK THIS COMPUTER
OR ADVERTISE "SPACE FOR RENT"

TO KNOW ALL, IT IS NECESSARY TO KNOW VERY LITTLE;
BUT TO KNOW THAT VERY LITTLE, ONE MUST FIRST
KNOW PRETTY MUCH.
                              - GEORGES I. GURDJIEFF
                                      (1872-1949)

INFINITY KNOWS

OFTEN REACHING BACK THROUGH TIME
FOR MEMORIES OF A FRIEND
DIVING DEEP, RETRIEVING
MOMENTS RIDING ON THE WIND

LIFETIMES SPENT TOGETHER
CREATE A CHERISHED BOND
HEARTS FOREVER LINKED
LIKE FLOWING RIPPLES IN A POND

A PROMISE SPRINGS ETERNAL
BETWEEN THE SOULS OF TWO
INFINITY KNOWS
I'LL ALWAYS BE THERE FOR YOU

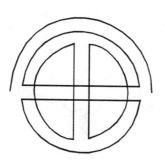

THE WIND BLOWS OVER THE LAKE AND STIRS THE
SURFACE OF THE WATER. THUS, VISIBLE EFFECTS OF
THE INVISIBLE ARE MANIFEST.
— I CHING

SMILE HIGH

GAZING AT THE NIGHTTIME SKY
I TILT MY HEAD AND SEE
A SMILE PEEKING THROUGH THE CLOUDS
HER LUMINOUS FACE WANING

AS POWER DRAWS ME TO THE SPOT
WHERE THE SUN SAT AT NOON
I CLOSE MY EYES AND IN A FLASH
I'M HALFWAY TO THE MOON

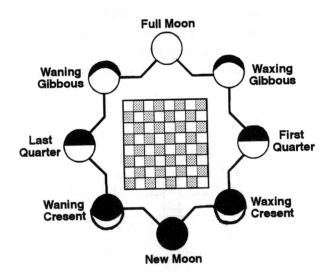

DOUBTING THOMASS

IF WE CAN LOOK INTO THE UNIVERSE
DOUBTING EXISTENCE OF WORTH
EQUALITY MIRRORS THE QUESTION
IS THERE INTELLIGENT LIFE ON EARTH

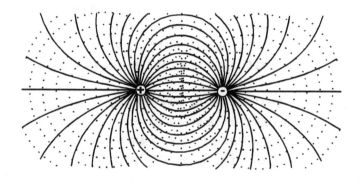

DOUBT IS A PAIN TOO LONELY TO KNOW THAT FAITH IS
HIS TWIN BROTHER.
- KAHLIL GIBRAN
THE PROPHET

WHAT IF

A TREE STANDS ALONE IN THE FOREST
LOVE BIRDS FORGET THEIR SONG
A POND SHOWS NO REFLECTION
SOMETHING IS DESPERATELY WRONG

FLOWERS CEASE TO OPEN
CRYSTALS LOSE THEIR SHINE
POLLUTED SOIL GROWS PLASTIC
INSTEAD OF FRUIT UPON THE VINE

BREATHING SEEMS SO LABORED
THE SUN PLAYS HIDE AND SEEK
THE TIDE DISRUPTS ITS RHYTHM
ALL LIFEFORMS SEEM SO WEAK

RUSTED METAL SWEEPS THE FLOOR
WHERE ONCE SWAM SCHOOLS OF FISH
IT'S MUCH LATER THAN WE KNOW
CAN'T YOU HEAR HER DYING WISH

SPACE TRAVEL INTRIGUES US
WILL WE SPREAD OUR GREED AND HATE
TO OTHERS OF COSMIC CONTRAST
WHAT WILL BECOME OUR PLANET'S FATE

LET OTHERS STRAIN TO CLEAN THE MESS
I'LL JUST CLOSE MY EYES
AND CHOOSE THE COMFORT OF ILLUSION
I'LL BET THESE HORROR STORIES ARE LIES

HER CONSTANT CRIES ARE FUTILE
THE BREAST HEAVES ONE LAST SIGH
HARD LABOR HAS TAKEN ITS TOLL
GIVING BIRTH THE MOTHER HAS DIED

THE PAST IS IN ITS GRAVE, 'THOUGH ITS GHOST
HAUNTS US.

       - ROBERT BROWNING

REPEATING ETERNITY

MY SOUL HAS BEEN SO MANY THINGS
A TIBETAN MONK, KNOWN EGYPTIAN KINGS,
SEEN THE DESERT, THE PRAIRIE, A CRYSTAL CAVE,
BEEN A SHAMAN, A HEALER AND EVEN A KNAVE

EXISTED SIMPLY ON THE AFRICAN PLAINS,
RIDDEN BAREBACK WITH THE WIND AS MY REINS
LIVED IN MERRY OLE ENGLAND, THE MOUNTAINS OF PERU,
KNOWN ANCIENT ATLANTIS AND EVEN MU

NOT TO MENTION MY CURRENT SPIRITUAL LIFE
PURSUING THE DREAM AS A MOTHER AND WIFE
WITH A WEALTH OF KNOWLEDGE FROM WHICH TO PICK
I HAVE THE FREEDOM TO FIND OUT WHAT MAKES ME TICK

THERE ARE NO GRAVES HERE. THESE MOUNTAINS AND
PLAINS ARE A CRADLE AND A STEPPING STONE.
WHENEVER YOU PASS BY THE FIELD WHERE YOU HAVE
LAID YOUR ANCESTORS, LOOK WELL THERE-UPON, AND
YOU SHALL SEE YOURSELVES AND YOUR CHILDREN
DANCING HAND IN HAND.

- KAHLIL GIBRAN
THE PROPHET

THE RAINBOW AND THE STORM

ENERGY ITSELF IS NOT EVIL
IT STARTS OUT PURE IN FORM
POWER DEPENDS ON HOW IT IS USED
THE RAINBOW IS PART OF THE STORM

POTENCY LIVES IN WHAT WE FEAR
AS WE FILL OUR CONTAINERS WITH LOVE
AND CHOOSE TO BATHE DAILY IN THE LIGHT
WE BECOME ONE WITH THE DOVE

LET THE SOUL OF MAN TAKE THE WHOLE UNIVERSE
FOR ITS BODY.
— SIMONE WEIL

INDIAN APARTHEID

BECAUSE WE DIDN'T UNDERSTAND
THEIR RELIGION AND CONNECTION TO EARTH
WE DROVE THEM ONTO BARREN LANDS
WHERE THEY WOULD NEVER QUENCH THEIR THIRST

THEY DIDN'T POLLUTE OR RAPE THEIR OWN MOTHER
LOOK WHAT'S HAPPENED TO THIS LAND THAT THEY NURSED
LET US FINALLY ACKNOWLEDGE THEIR WISDOM AND
STRENGTH
THESE TRUE AMERICANS WHO WERE HERE FIRST

WE'VE DECRIED WHAT'S HAPPENED IN OTHER LANDS
SOUTH AFRICA AND GERMANY WHERE MANY HAVE DIED
IS IT SAVAGE TO TRY TO SAVE YOUR OWN HOME
ARE WE STILL BLIND TO INDIAN APARTHEID

GREAT SPIRITS HAVE ALWAYS ENCOUNTERED VIOLENT
OPPOSITION FROM MEDIOCRE MINDS.
                                    - ALBERT EINSTEIN

THE GUARDIAN

PEACE TALKS IN OHIO
WHO WOULD HAVE EVER GUESSED
DOES WRIGHT PATTERSON HOLD THE KEY
HAVE ITS SECRETS BEEN UNDRESSED

WHAT WAS REVEALED TO THOSE WHO MET
TO HELP CHOOSE A WORLD OF PEACE
DID ALIEN TECHNOLOGY
CONVINCE THAT WAR MUST FINALLY CEASE

WE MUST LEARN TO LIVE IN HARMONY
WITH NATURE AS WELL AS MAN
OR SUFFER SEVERE REPERCUSSIONS
FROM THE GUARDIAN COSMIC HAND

THE FATES LEAD HIM WHO WILL - HIM WHO WON'T,
THEY DRAG.
- SENECA

THE COLOR OF THE FUTURE

THE CHILDREN ARE OUR FUTURE
THEY'LL INHERIT THIS EARTH
IT'S IMPORTANT THAT THEY KNOW OF LOVE
FROM THE MOMENT OF THEIR BIRTH

TREAT ALL CHILDREN EQUALLY
NO MATTER WHAT THEIR RACE
YOU CANNOT JUDGE WHAT LIES INSIDE
BY THE COLOR OF THEIR FACE

THE FUTURE WILL BE CREATED BY EACH ONE OF US. LET US ALL ANTICIPATE AND PREPARE, EVEN CELEBRATE OUR JOURNEY TOWARD NEW REALITIES OF LIFE.

- RAINBOW EAGLE

BORN AGAIN, AGAIN, AND AGAIN

DEATH AND REBIRTH OCCUR EACH DAY
IT'S A GIFT GIVEN TO MAN
WE HONOR THE PAST, BUT LOOK FORWARD
TO THE BIRTH OF THE MOMENT AT HAND

THE CYCLE OF LIFE IS MERELY A CIRCLE
THE BEGINNING AND END ARE THE SAME
IT MATTERS NOT WHETHER WE WIN OR LOSE
BUT HOW WE PLAY THE GAME

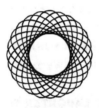

EVERYTHING THE POWER OF THE WORLD DOES IS DONE IN A CIRCLE. THE SKY IS ROUND, AND I HAVE HEARD THAT THE EARTH IS ROUND LIKE A BALL, AND SO ARE ALL THE STARS. THE WIND, IN ITS GREATEST POWER, WHIRLS. BIRDS MAKE THEIR NESTS IN CIRCLES, FOR THEIRS IS THE SAME RELIGION AS OURS. THE SUN COMES FORTH AND GOES DOWN AGAIN IN A CIRCLE. THE MOON DOES THE SAME, AND BOTH ARE ROUND. EVEN THE SEASONS FORM A GREAT CIRCLE IN THEIR CHANGING...THE LIFE OF MAN IS A CIRCLE FROM CHILDHOOD TO CHILDHOOD, AND SO IT IS IN EVERYTHING WHERE POWER MOVES. OUR TEPEES WERE ROUND LIKE THE NESTS OF BIRDS, AND WERE ALWAYS SET IN A CIRCLE, THE NATION'S HOOP, A NEST OF MANY NESTS, WHERE THE GREAT SPIRIT MEANT FOR US TO HATCH OUR CHILDREN.

- BLACK ELK

GOD'S MANY FACES

A BLADE OF GRASS, A BABBLING BROOK
UNINTERRUPTED TIME TO READ A BOOK
THE SMELL OF FLOWERS IN THE AIR
THE JOY OF EATING A JUICY PEAR

THE SIGHT OF A HAWK SOARING HIGH
WATCHING DANCING STARS IN A BLACKENED SKY
SEEING A PET DO SOMETHING CUTE
LIKE TRYING TO GET INSIDE YOUR BOOT

THE GAS TANK IS FULL WHEN YOU GET IN THE CAR
FOR THE VERY FIRST TIME, YOU GOLFED PAR
NONE OF THE SOCKS IN YOUR DRAWER ARE TORN
YOUR FUTURE IN-LAWS DON'T HAVE HORNS

SPONTANEOUS LAUGHTER WITH A FRIEND
A GARDEN THAT YOU LOVINGLY TEND
GIVING A GIFT FOR NO REASON AT ALL
TAKING TIME OUT TO HAVE A BALL

THE AUTUMN COLORS OF A TREE
THE BUSY WORKINGS OF A BEE
A GENUINE SMILE THAT MELTS YOUR HEART
SOMEONE ELSE RETURNING YOUR GROCERY CART

THE FIRST FLOWER OF SPRING PEEKING UP FROM THE
GROUND
SOMETHING LOST IS FINALLY FOUND
YOUR COLLEGE STUDENT CALLS AND DOESN'T WANT MONEY
GEE, THIS FEELING SURE IS FUNNY

A SMALL CHILD'S HUG AROUND YOUR LEG
THE TUB IS CLEAN WITHOUT HAVING TO BEG
THE GENTLE SOUNDS OF A FAVORITE TUNE
THE BRILLIANCE OF A BIG ORANGE MOON

A GLORIOUS SUNRISE OUT OF THE BLUE
A GIFT OF THE MOMENT, IT'S BRAND NEW
THE ENCHANTMENT OF WONDER IN SO MANY PLACES
IS ONLY A FEW OF GOD'S MANY FACES

IT'S A FUNNY THING ABOUT LIFE; IF YOU REFUSE TO
ACCEPT ANYTHING BUT THE BEST, YOU OFTEN GET IT.
- W. SOMERSET MAUGHAM

REALITY CHECK

CRYSTAL CAVES, ANGELIC BEINGS
WHAT GIFTS OF WONDER ARE YOU SEEING
ADVENTURE GREETS THE LIGHT OF DAY
IN SIMPLE AND CREATIVE WAYS

VIBRATION LIVES IN MANY STATES
AND WINDS DOWN PATHS THROUGH MANY GATES
WHAT IS REAL AND WHAT'S PRETEND
WHAT SHAPE AND COLOR IS THE WIND

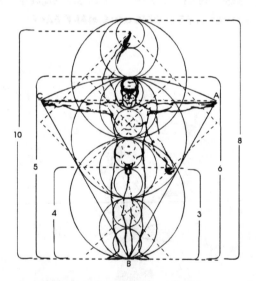

THE DISTRIBUTION OF ENERGY FOLLOWS DEFINITE
PATHS WHICH MAY BE STUDIED BY MEANS OF
GEOMETRIC CONSTRUCTION.
                                    - SAMUEL COLMAN

PHOTOGRAPH OF CLOUD TAKEN BY THE AUTHOR ON MARCH 21, 1996, IN NOLO, THE YUCATAN AT THE HOME OF A LOCAL ELDER IMMEDIATELY AFTER A PLANETARY HEALING CEREMONY.

AND IN THE SHIFTING OF THE WINDS, AND IN THE CLOUDS THAT ARE PRESSED INTO SERVICE BETWIXT HEAVEN AND EARTH, ARE SIGNS TO PEOPLE WHO CAN UNDERSTAND.

- KORAN

25

SMALL WONDER

THERE'S WONDER IN ALL OF NATURE
EVEN DOWN TO THE TINIEST BUG
WHY MUST WE STOMP AND SMACK AND KILL
BECAUSE IT'S CRAWLING ON OUR RUG

EACH LIFEFORM HAS A PURPOSE
WHETHER WE REALIZE IT OR NOT
HOW WOULD YOU LIKE TO BE MAIMED OR KILLED
'CAUSE YOU DROVE DOWN THE WRONG BLOCK

PRACTICE UNCONDITIONAL LOVE
OF LIFE IN ALL ITS FORMS
KINDLY PUT THE BUG OUTSIDE
COMPASSION KEEPS THE HEART WARM

REALIZING THAT VISIBLE BODIES ARE ONLY SYMBOLS
OF INVISIBLE FORCES, THE ANCIENTS WORSHIPPED
THE DIVINE POWER THROUGH THE LOWER KINGDOMS
OF NATURE...THE SAGES OF OLD STUDIED LIVING
THINGS TO A POINT OF REALIZATION THAT GOD IS
MOST PERFECTLY UNDERSTOOD THROUGH A
KNOWLEDGE OF HIS SUPREME HANDIWORK... ANIMATE
AND INANIMATE NATURE. EVERY EXISTING CREATURE
MANIFESTS SOME ASPECT OF THE INTELLIGENCE OR
POWER OF THE ETERNAL ONE.

- MANLY P. HALL
THE SECRET TEACHINGS OF ALL AGES

THE FACE ON THE PLATE

DO YOU KNOW HOW THE FOOD YOU EAT IS RAISED
THAT YOU'RE EATING VIBRATIONS OF FEAR
ARE YOU AWARE OF THE INHUMANE LIVING CONDITIONS
OF PIGS, SHEEP, CHICKEN AND STEER

WHY MUST WE CONTINUE TO EAT FOOD THAT HAS FACES
WHEN THERE'S PLENTY TO CHOOSE FROM THE LAND
WILL WE ONE DAY CONSUME THE FLESH
CURRENTLY KNOWN AS MAN

...AND THE FRUIT SHALL BE FOR MEAT, AND THE LEAF
THEREOF FOR MEDICINE.
- EZEKIEL 47:12

AND GOD SAID, "BEHOLD, I HAVE GIVEN YOU EVERY
HERB BEARING SEED, WHICH IS UPON THE FACE OF
THE EARTH, AND EVERY TREE, IN WHICH IS THE FRUIT
OF A TREE YIELDING SEED; TO YOU IT SHALL BE FOR
MEAT."
- GENESIS 1:29

LIVING THE DREAM

WHAT WOULD YOU CHOOSE TO DO
IF YOU KNEW YOU WOULDN'T FAIL
WE'RE TALKING ABOUT THOSE PASSIONS
THAT WON'T LAND YOUR SOUL IN JAIL

WOULD YOU BECOME A MUSICIAN OR PAINTER,
DIG AN ARCHEOLOGICAL SITE,
START YOUR OWN BUSINESS, TRAVEL THE WORLD,
SAIL THE WIND ON THE WINGS OF A KITE

THE DECISION TO START IS THE HARD PART
YOU KNOW WHAT YOU HAVE TO DO
WITH DESIRE AND EFFORT AND BELIEF IN YOURSELF
YOUR DREAMS REALLY CAN COME TRUE

TWO DEJECTED ASSISTANTS OF THOMAS EDISON SAID:
"WE'VE JUST COMPLETED OUR SEVEN HUNDREDTH
EXPERIMENT AND WE STILL DON'T HAVE THE ANSWER.
WE HAVE FAILED."
"NO, MY FRIENDS, YOU HAVEN'T FAILED" REPLIED MR.
EDISON. "IT'S JUST THAT WE KNOW MORE ABOUT THIS
SUBJECT THAN ANYONE ELSE ALIVE. AND WE'RE
CLOSER TO FINDING THE ANSWER, BECAUSE NOW WE
KNOW SEVEN HUNDRED THINGS NOT TO DO. DON'T
CALL IT A MISTAKE. CALL IT AN EDUCATION.

THE LIGHT AT THE END OF THE TUNNEL

WOULDN'T IT BE A GREAT BIG HOAX
TO FIND OUT IN THE END
THAT WHAT WAS FEARED ALL ALONG
WAS LOVE COMING 'ROUND THE BEND

THE LIGHT AT THE END OF THE TUNNEL
IS NOT ALWAYS AN ONCOMING TRAIN
OPEN YOUR MIND TO NEW CONCEPTS
FRESH AIR IS GOOD FOR THE BRAIN

THINGS DO NOT CHANGE; WE CHANGE.
- HENRY DAVID THOREAU

PERSECUTION COMPLEX

FLAMES LICKING THE FINGER TIPS
WELDING THE CHAINS THAT BIND
RELEASE A PERSECUTED SOUL
ONE MORE TIME

UNHEARD CRIES RETREAT WITHIN
AS EVAPORATED TEARS
DOUSE A SEA OF FIRE
RAINING SILENCE LOUD AND CLEAR

TELEPATHIC MESSAGES,
A HEALING SENSE OF TOUCH,
KNOWLEDGE OF UNSEEN REALMS
FOR SOME IT'S ALL TOO MUCH

FOLLOW ME, THUNDERS THE VOICE
HELLO, MY NAME IS FEAR
I'LL GLADLY DO YOUR THINKING
AND TELL YOU WHAT YOU WANT TO HEAR

OPPRESSION'S STILL ALIVE AND WELL
IN THOSE WHO FAIL TO SEE
THAT USE OF EXTRASENSORY GIFTS
IS PART OF MAN'S DESTINY

WHAT IS THAT DESTINY
SOUL KNOWS IT'S ESSENTIAL
TO CHIP AWAY THE FEAR
AND BECOME OUR POTENTIAL

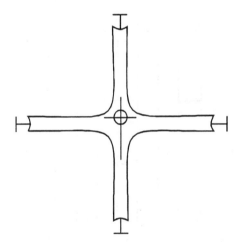

HIDING IN PLAIN SIGHT

I CONSTANTLY SEARCH TO FIND THE TRUTH
WONDERING WHERE IT COULD POSSIBLY BE
TIME REVEALED ITS HIDING PLACE
RIGHT INSIDE OF ME

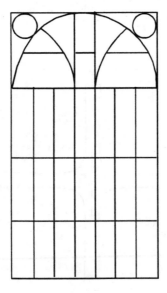

MEN STUMBLE OVER THE TRUTH FROM TIME TO TIME,
BUT MOST PICK THEMSELVES UP AND HURRY OFF AS IF
NOTHING HAPPENED.
                                    - SIR WINSTON CHURCHILL

MAN ON THE MOON

SCIENTISTS SEEM TO MEAN WELL
IN THEIR POUNDING QUEST FOR PROOF
THE WORLD WAS FLAT NOT LONG AGO
WHAT'LL BE TOMORROW'S SPOOF

THOUGH SCIENCE IS EVER CHANGING
WE'RE STILL BOUND BY WHAT WE KNOW
A MAN ON THE MOON, WHO WOULD HAVE THOUGHT
ONE HUNDRED YEARS AGO

ONE WHO SPEAKS THE TRUTH IS NOT NECESSARILY
TRUTH ITSELF. JUST AS ONE WHO POINTS AT THE SUN IS
NOT THE SUN.

- TED ANDREWS
ANIMAL SPEAK

COURAGE REMEMBERED

CONSIDERING THOSE WHO LOOK LIKE ME
FOR CENTURIES BETRAYED
THE NATIVE AMERICAN PEOPLE
BREAKING MANY PROMISES MADE

WHAT GAVE YOU THE COURAGE
TO OPENLY TRUST AGAIN
AND SHARE YOUR HEART AND LAND
SO THAT HEALING COULD BEGIN

AS YOU LOOKED INTO OUR EYES
TO THE DEPTHS OF THE SOUL
DID YOU SEE THAT WE WANT PEACE
AND OUR MOTHER MADE WHOLE

WE CAME BACK TO ASSIST
EVERY RACE IS REPRESENTED
AND WILL PROUDLY WALK BESIDE YOU
UNTIL ALL DIFFERENCES ARE MENDED

I REMEMBER YOU FROM LONG AGO
WHEN YOUR SPIRIT RODE THE WIND
YOU'VE RETURNED A RAINBOW WARRIOR
RIDING FREEDOM ONCE AGAIN

IT'S AT TIMES A LONELY JOURNEY
AND DISTRACTION TAKES ITS TOLL
BUT THE BATTLE CAN'T BE LOST
THEY WILL NEVER OWN OUR SOUL

WE'VE ALL BEEN HERE MANY LIFETIMES
SEEMING NEVER TO BELONG
NOW OUR ESSENCE BLENDS TOGETHER
BEATING AS ONE HEART, ONE SONG

A PERSON TOO WRAPPED UP IN HIMSELF MAKES A
SMALL PACKAGE.
                                    - STANDING ELK

THE HAND OF FATE

HEADING TOWARD DEATH
THE EMOTIONS I FELT
WERE PEACE AND ACCEPTANCE
OF THE HAND I'D BEEN DEALT

ON AN ICY HIGHWAY
AS MY CAR FOUGHT
IT LOST TO AN 18 WHEELER
IN A "WELCOME AREA" PARKING LOT

THE GUARDIAN ANGELS
ON DUTY THAT DAY
MEAN MORE
THAN I CAN EVER CONVEY

THE CHANCE TO RETURN
FROM THIS PLACE BEYOND FEAR
HELPS GUIDE AND DEFINE
A PURPOSE NOW CLEAR

TRANSCENDENTAL JOURNEY

THE PLAYGROUND OF THE ANGELS
IS A REALM OF SHIMMERING LIGHT
OFTENTIMES WHILE STEALING SILENCE
THEIR APPEARANCE FLICKERS BRIGHT

ON MY TRANSCENDENTAL JOURNEY
I WATCH THEIR PRISMS DANCE
HOW FORTUNATE MY LIFE HAS BEEN
TO HAVE EXPERIENCED THIS CHANCE

THE WORLDS ORIGINATE SO THAT TRUTH MAY COME
AND DWELL THEREIN.
                                        - BUDDHA

THE KINDNESS OF STRANGERS

HOW CAN WE WATCH ON THE NEWS EACH NIGHT
THE DESTRUCTION AND FAMINE IN LANDS
WHERE POVERTY RULES AND SURVIVAL DEPENDS
UPON STRANGERS' HEARTS AND HANDS

WE MUST NOT BECOME COMPLACENT
SIMPLY IGNORING ALL THE FUSS
DISASTERS DON'T HAPPEN ONLY TO OTHERS
WHO WILL HELP WHEN IT HAPPENS TO US

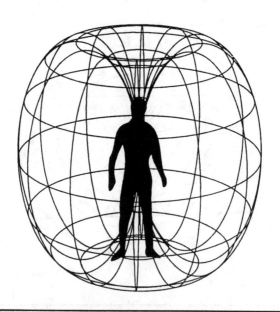

HARMONY MAKES SMALL THINGS GROW. LACK OF IT
MAKES GREAT THINGS DECAY.
- SALLUST (C 86-34 B.C.)
ROMAN HISTORIAN AND POLITICIAN

HIDDEN POTENTIAL

THE POTENTIAL
OF THE MIGHTY OAK

LIES WITHIN
THE ACORN'S CLOAK

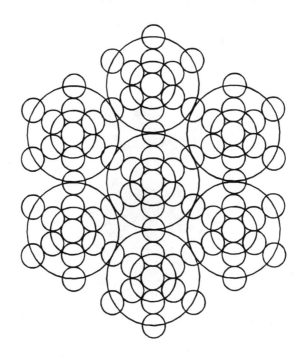

THERE IS NO HEAVIER BURDEN THAN A GREAT
POTENTIAL.
                                    - CHARLIE BROWN

ROSEBUD

DON'T BELIEVE ANOTHER'S TRUTH
WITHOUT CHEWING YOUR OWN CUD
IN TIME, A FLOWER REVEALS ITSELF
A ROSE STARTS AS A BUD

YOU'LL RECOGNIZE TRUTH WHEN YOU HEAR IT
IT'S NOT BASED ON WHAT YOU LEARN
BELIEVE IT OR NOT ALMOST ALWAYS
IT'S BASED ON WHAT YOU UN-LEARN

LIVE YOUR BELIEFS AND YOU CAN TURN THE WORLD
AROUND.
                              - HENRY DAVID THOREAU

EGO'S FOE

WHEN THERE'S SOMETHING WE DON'T UNDERSTAND
WE OFTEN LIVE IN FEAR
DENY THAT IT COULD BE A TRUTH
THAT OTHERS WANT TO HEAR

A FUNNY THING THE EGO
IT'S QUICK TO CHOOSE A FOE
NEW CONCEPTS SURELY HAVE NO WORTH
IF EGO DOESN'T KNOW

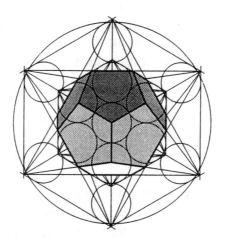

WHOEVER UNDERTAKES TO SET HIMSELF UP AS A
JUDGE IN THE FIELD OF TRUTH AND KNOWLEDGE IS
SHIPWRECKED BY THE LAUGHTER OF THE GODS.

- ALBERT EINSTEIN

EVERYBODY'S TRAGEDY

ONE BUILDING - DEVASTATION
GLASS SLICES THE AIR
SCREAMS OF PANIC, SILENT STARES
MILLIONS WHO INSTANTLY CARE

CHILDREN SLEEPING, NOW WEEPING
WANT THEIR MOMS AND DADS
MANY REST ETERNAL
A SAGA UNBEARABLY SAD

STRANGERS BROUGHT TOGETHER
THROUGH A GHOULISH DREAM AWOKEN
THE POWER OF LOVE PROVES PAINFULLY
THE HUMAN SPIRIT CAN'T BE BROKEN

MAN DESTROYING HIS FELLOWMAN
BY PERSUASION OF A BOMB
THE AGONY OF ONE MOMENT
BRINGS HOME BAGHDAD AND VIETNAM

CAN DISASTER BECOME A SYMBOL
A CATALYST FOR CHANGE
SO THAT BAYLEE AND OTHERS WILL KNOW
THAT THEIR DEATHS WERE NOT IN VAIN

ALL OF LIFE IS CONNECTED
EACH WITH IMPORTANT GIFTS TO GIVE
HOW MIGHT HAVE OUR WORLD BEEN DIFFERENT
IF ONE OF THE VICTIMS HAD LIVED

LOOSE SCREWS

WHAT IS THIS SPARK OF PURE BRIGHT LIGHT
CONTAINED WITHIN EACH BEING
DO OTHERS SOMETIMES FEEL CONFUSED
AS TO WHAT THEY THINK THEY'RE SEEING

HOW MANY OFTEN WISH
THIS WAS ALL A BUNCH OF BUNK
THAT THEY'D NEVER HEARD OF THEIR THIRD EYE
OR HAD A PAST LIFE AS A MONK

HANG IN THERE FRIEND, THE WORD IS OUT
MANY ARE NOW ON THE SAME QUEST
OUR SCREWS ARE NOT LOOSE OR SET TIGHTER
WE CHOSE A DIFFERENT PATH FOR OUR TESTS

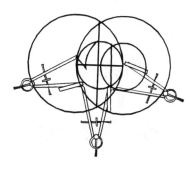

A CRANK IS A MAN WITH A NEW IDEA - UNTIL IT
CATCHES ON.
                                    - MARK TWAIN

FRAGMENTS

WE SEARCH WITHIN TO FIND OURSELVES
DISCOVER FRAGMENTS OF THE WHOLE
THE FEAR, THE LOVE, THE UGLINESS
ALL VYING FOR A STARRING ROLE

LEARN WHO YOU ARE, BEFRIEND EACH PIECE
THERE WAS JOY BEFORE THE FALL
IN TIME A MIRACLE WILL UNFOLD
HUMPTY DUMPTY IS WHOLE UPON THE WALL

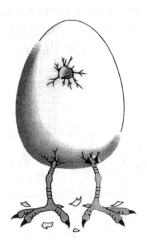

ANYONE WHO DOESN'T BELIEVE IN MIRACLES IS NOT A REALIST.
                                        - DAVID BEN-GURION

THE IMPORTANCE OF CHOICES

ARE WE CHOSEN OR DID WE CHOOSE
BECAUSE OF LOVE AND COMPASSION
TO SERVE ANOTHER LIFE SENTENCE
ON THIS PLANET OF DUALITY

THOUGH CAPABLE OF PLAYING ANY ROLE
IN THIS GRAND COSMIC PLAY
SELF DIRECTION OF CIRCUMSTANCE HAS TAUGHT
THE IMPORTANCE OF CHOICES

ARE WE CHOSEN OR DID WE CHOOSE
TO SHARE OUR GIFTS AND TALENTS
AS WE CIRCLE AGAIN THIS WHEEL OF LIFE
MAYBE WE CHOSE TO BE CHOSEN

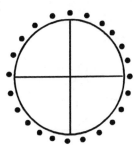

MIND IS THE MASTER POWER THAT MOULDS AND
MAKES, AND MAN IS MIND, AND EVERMORE HE TAKES
THE TOOL OF THOUGHT, AND SHAPING WHAT HE
WILLS, BRINGS FORTH A THOUSAND JOYS, A THOUSAND
ILLS.
— JAMES ALLEN

GRADUATION DAY

IS ONE OF OUR EARTHLY LESSONS
LEARNING HOW FAR FROM SOURCE WE CAN GO
THEN, MANY WILL EASILY GRADUATE
WITH A GOLD FRAMED DIPLOMA IN TOW

THE RETURN HOME CAN BE A STRUGGLE
WHEN WE STRAY A LITTLE TOO FAR
IT CAN ALSO BE WELL WORTH THE EFFORT
WHEN OUR VOYAGE IS LIT BY THE STARS

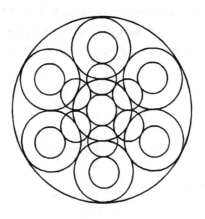

THERE IS A GOD WHO KNOWS AND LOVES US. AND GOD
LOVES US EVEN THOUGH GOD KNOWS US.
- GREG ANDERSON
THE CANCER CONQUEROR

BLESSINGS

SOME BLESSINGS IN LIFE
COME DISGUISED AS WRATH
TO HELP US LEARN OUR LESSONS
AND ADVANCE THE SPIRITUAL PATH

MUCH GROWTH COMES THROUGH ADVERSITY,
SOMETIMES WE MUST ENDURE
WHEN POSSIBLE, SEE THE HUMOR
IT CAN BE A MIRACLE CURE

THOUGH GRATEFUL FOR EACH TEACHING
THEIR WORTH WE COMPREHEND
RELEASE THOSE LEARNED WITH LIGHT AND LOVE
TO NEVER EXPERIENCE AGAIN

BE KIND, FOR EVERYONE YOU MEET IS FACING A HARD BATTLE.
                                        - PLATO

PLAYFUL HEART

DOES FASCINATION WITH LIFE
SOMETIMES GET LEFT BEHIND
WHEN WE GROW INTO ADULTHOOD
AND BECOME OBSESSED WITH OUR MIND

PUT ASIDE SERIOUSNESS
OPEN THE HEART TO PLAY
REMEMBER CAREFREE, YOUTHFUL TIMES
CREATING JOY IN SIMPLE WAYS

RECAPTURE CHILDLIKE WONDER
IT'S NEVER TO LATE
ALLOW SOME TIME FOR FUN EACH DAY
SPONTANEITY CAN'T WAIT

IF THE MIND IS NOT CONTRIVED, IT IS SPONTANEOUSLY
BLISSFUL. JUST AS WATER, WHEN NOT AGITATED, IS BY
NATURE TRANSPARENT AND CLEAR.

— THE TIBETAN BOOK OF LIVING AND DYING

UNION OF THE CIRCLE AND THE SQUARE

STRAIGHT, SQUARE, GREAT, WITHOUT PURPOSE, YET NOTHING REMAINS UNFURTHERED. THE SYMBOL OF HEAVEN IS THE CIRCLE, AND THAT OF EARTH IS THE SQUARE. THUS SQUARENESS IS A PRIMARY QUALITY OF THE EARTH. ON THE OTHER HAND, MOVEMENT IN A STRAIGHT LINE, AS WELL AS MAGNITUDE, IS A PRIMARY QUALITY OF THE CREATIVE. BUT ALL SQUARE THINGS HAVE THEIR ORIGIN IN A STRAIGHT LINE AND IN TURN FORM SOLID BODIES. IN MATHEMATICS, WHEN WE DISCRIMINATE BETWEEN LINES, PLANES, AND SOLIDS, WE FIND THAT RECTANGULAR PLANES RESULT FROM STRAIGHT LINES, AND CUBIC MAGNITUDES FROM RECTANGULAR PLANES. THE RECEPTIVE ACCOMMODATES ITSELF TO THE QUALITIES OF THE CREATIVE AND MAKES THEM ITS OWN. THUS A SQUARE DEVELOPS OUT OF A STRAIGHT LINE, AND A CUBE OUT OF A SQUARE. THIS IS COMPLIANCE WITH THE LAWS OF THE CREATIVE; NOTHING IS TAKEN AWAY, NOTHING ADDED. THEREFORE THE RECEPTIVE HAS NO NEED OF A SPECIAL PURPOSE OF ITS OWN, NOR OF ANY EFFORT; YET EVERYTHING TURNS OUT AS IT SHOULD.

NATURE CREATES ALL BEINGS WITHOUT ERRING: THIS IS ITS STRAIGHTNESS. IT IS CALM AND STILL; THIS IS ITS FOURSQUARENESS. IT TOLERATES ALL CREATURES EQUALLY; THIS IS ITS GREATNESS. THEREFORE IT ATTAINS WHAT IS RIGHT FOR ALL WITHOUT ARTIFICE OR SPECIAL INTENTIONS. MAN ACHIEVES THE HEIGHT OF WISDOM WHEN ALL THAT HE DOES IS AS SELF-EVIDENT AS WHAT NATURE DOES.

- 2ND HEXAGRAM,
"THE RECEPTIVE,"
THE I CHING

THE SILENT DRUM

THE HEARTBEAT OF OUR MOTHER
IS CONTAINED WITHIN THE DRUM
WITH HER DYING BREATH SHE WANTS TO KNOW
WHERE ALL THE POLLUTION CAME FROM

TOXIC WASTE, RAPING THE LAND
WE'VE MANIFESTED HER WORST FEARS
SHE'S AWAKENED FROM A NIGHTMARE
CHOKING BACK A TRAIL OF TEARS

WHAT ARE WE DOING TO OUR PLANET
WITH SO LITTLE REGARD WE DESTROY HER FACE
TO CONTINUE ALONG THIS MINDLESS PATH
WILL GUARANTEE THE IMPERMANENCE OF THE HUMAN RACE

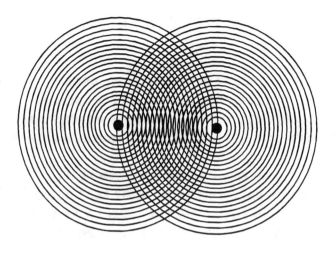

I REALIZE THE ULTIMATE DESTINY OF MY PEOPLE.
THEY WILL BE EXTIRPATED BY THE RACE THAT
OVERRUNS, OCCUPIES AND HOLDS OUR HUNTING
GROUNDS, WHOSE NUMBERS AND FORCE, WITH THE
GOVERNMENT AND MILLIONS BEHIND IT WILL IN A FEW
YEARS REMOVE THE LAST TRACE OF OUR BLOOD THAT
NOW REMAINS. WE SHALL FALL AS THE LEAVES FROM
THE TREES WHEN FROST OR WINTER COMES AND THE
LANDS WHICH WE HAVE ROAMED OVER FOR
COUNTLESS GENERATIONS WILL BE GIVEN OVER TO
THE MINER AND THE PLOWSHARE. IN PLACE OF OUR
HUMBLE TEPEES, THE "WHITE MAN'S" TOWNS AND
CITIES WILL APPEAR AND WE SHALL BE BURIED OUT
OF SIGHT BENEATH THE AVALANCHE OF THE NEW
CIVILIZATION. THIS IS THE DESTINY OF MY PEOPLE.
MY PART IS TO PROTECT THEM AND YOURS AS FAR AS
I CAN, FROM THE VIOLENCE AND BLOODSHED WHILE I
LIVE, AND TO BRING BOTH INTO FRIENDLY RELATIONS,
SO THAT THEY MAY BE AT PEACE WITH ONE ANOTHER.

PARAPHRASED BY A REPORTER,
THE PHILOSOPHY OF UTE CHIEF OURAY
LATE 1800'S

A VERY OLD FRIEND

ONCE AT NIGHT WITHIN MY DREAM
INSTEAD OF RELEASING A SILENT SCREAM
UPON MEETING AN OLD BROWN WRINKLY MAN
I LET LOVE REPLACE FEAR AS I TOUCHED HIS HAND

OVERWHELMING LOVE AND PEACE
SURROUNDED THIS BEING AS MY FEAR RELEASED
AS HIS LOVING ENERGY TOUCHED MY ARM
I KNEW THIS OLD FRIEND WOULD DO NO HARM

IN THIS REALITY, PLANET EARTH WILL ULTIMATELY
FIND HER PLACE AMONG THE STARS AND WE WILL
BECOME PREPARED TO GROW TOWARD THE
PLANETARY FAMILY.
                                    - RAINBOW EAGLE

RESPECT YOUR ELDERS

WE EMBRACE AND REVER MODERN KNOWLEDGE
BELIEVING NEW IS BETTER THAN OLD
ONE OF THESE DAYS WE'll REALIZE
THAT WHAT'S SHINY IS NOT ALWAYS GOLD

RESPECT THE PATH OF YOUR ELDERS
HONORING GRANDMOTHERS AND GRANDFATHERS
THEIR PEARLS OF WISDOM ARE PRICELESS
HINDSIGHT WILL REJOICE THAT YOU BOTHERED

WISDOM SHOULD BE CHERISHED AS A MEANS OF
TRAVELING FROM YOUTH TO OLD AGE, FOR IT IS MORE
LASTING THAN ANY OTHER POSSESSION.
- BIAS OF PRIENE (C. 570 B.C.)
(ONE OF THE SEVEN SAGES OF ANCIENT GREECE)

DO NOT SEEK TO FOLLOW THE FOOTSTEPS OF THE
MEN OF OLD; SEEK WHAT THEY SOUGHT.
- MATSUO BASHO (1644-1694)
JAPANESE POET

SELF-LOVE

IN LEARNING TO LOVE YOURSELF
A SHIMMERING LIGHT SHINES THROUGH
SHARE THIS GIFT WITH SINCERITY OF HEART
AND THE UNIVERSE WILL OPEN TO YOU

THE UNIVERSE IS THE EXTERNALIZATION OF THE SOUL.
- RALPH WALDO EMERSON

DANCE OF HARMONY

SOME REMAIN SEPARATE FROM THE WHOLE
BECAUSE OF SOCIAL OR RACIAL PRIDE
AND THROUGH IGNORANCE HARM OUR ATMOSPHERE
GIVING BIGOTRY AND HATE A FREE RIDE

MAKE OUR PLANET A HOME OF LOVE
WHERE EACH SPARK OF LIFE HAS A CHANCE
TO BECOME THE PERFECT CREATION
IN HARMONY PERFORMING LIFE'S DANCE

IF YOU DO WHAT YOU'VE ALWAYS DONE, YOU'LL GET
WHAT YOU'VE ALWAYS GOTTEN.

ANONYMOUS

THE FINGER

INSTEAD OF POINTING THE FINGER
HIGHLIGHTING WHAT OTHERS DO
CONCENTRATE ON THE THREE
THAT ARE POINTING BACK AT YOU

THOUGH OTHERS HAVE FAULTS, CONCENTRATE ON
YOUR OWN.

- 365 TAO

MEDITATION

THE CONDUCTOR OF THE LIGHT
WAVES A MAGIC WAND TO START THE DAY
DANCING ON STREAMS OF ECSTASY
SHADOWS REFLECT HARMONIC RAYS

IRIDESCENT BEAMS DISPLAY
THEIR BRILLIANCE BEFORE CLOSED EYES
THE STILLNESS OF MEDITATIVE BLISS
WEAVES AN INTRICATE WEB OF COSMIC TIES

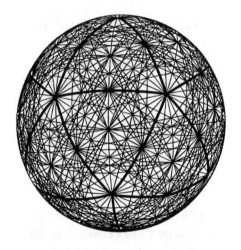

WHEN THE MIND BECOMES ATTUNED, IT BECOMES
CAPABLE OF HEARING THE VOICE OF THE UNKNOWN.
THE SOUNDS WHICH ARE HEARD IN SUCH A STATE DO
NOT BELONG TO ANY PARTICULAR LANGUAGE,
RELIGION OR TRADITION.

- SWAMI RAMA
MUSIC & SOUND IN HEALING ARTS
BY JOHN BEAULIEU

THE REALITY OF ILLUSION

GEOMETRIC SYMBOLS
APPEAR IN MY DREAMS
LOVING TINY BABIES
WISER THAN THEIR YEARS

SLOPING, LANDSCAPED HILLSIDES
TRAVELING ON A FUNNY BUS
STRANGERS SEEM FAMILIAR
SOME FACES DAZED AND LOST

TOURS OF THE NIGHT TIME SKY
TO GALAXIES UNKNOWN
SOMEPLACE NEAR POLARIS,
ANTARES AND ANDROMEDA

ROTATING COUNTER CLOCKWISE
WHAT DOES THAT MEAN
LANDING IN THE OCEAN
LIGHTS FLASHING, RESCUING

RETRIEVING BITS AND PIECES
IT DOESN'T MAKE MUCH SENSE
THE ONLY THING I FEAR
IS GETTING MOTION SICKNESS

RIDING IN A ROCKING CAR
IT'S REALLY HARD TO STEER
HEARING SOMEONE SAY
"JUST DRINK THIS ELIXIR"

BLUE LIGHTS DESCENDING
IN FRONT OF MY CAR
A JOLT INTO THE KIDNEY
AM I STUCK TO A TOWER

THE ROOF OF MY MOUTH IS GONE
THOUGHTS OF DNA
PRESENTED BALLS OF LIGHT
ALL INTEGRATE INTO MY DAY

TAKING TESTS IN CLASSROOMS
BEARS EXAMINING CATS
IN ONE DREAMTIME SCENARIO
A TALL MAN IN A CHIMNEY SWEEP HAT

SUCKED INTO SOME KIND OF TUBE
THE PRESSURE HURTS MY HEAD
SURGICAL PROCEDURES
ALL AT ONCE I'M BACK IN BED

A HUGE CLOUD FALLS RAPIDLY
ENGULFED IN NEEDLES AND PINS
RED DOTS STAIN MY BODY
WHAT IS REAL AND WHAT'S PRETEND

LYING ON A TABLE
REACHING OUT TO TOUCH A HAND
VIEWING EARTH FROM AFAR
SO MUCH LOVE FROM A BRONZETONE MAN

HIDING FROM AN ENEMY PLANE
IN A HILLSIDE BUNKER WITHOUT A DOOR
A BABY IN A PAN OF GEL
TRANSPORTED IN A DRESSER DRAWER

EQUATIONS I DON'T UNDERSTAND
IS THAT BRIGHT ORANGE BALL THE MOON
I GET UP TO TAKE A LOOK
AM I JUST ANOTHER LOON

MY TEACHER STANDS BEHIND ME
JUST OUT OF SIGHT
AND TELLS ME I'LL REMEMBER MORE
WHEN THE TIME IS RIGHT

WAKING UP AT 4:15
THERE'S MUCH IN MY HEAD
I TELL MYSELF NOT TO FORGET
OH, WHAT WAS THAT HE SAID

INAUDIBLE TO OUR DEAF MORTAL EARS THE WIDE
WORLD-RHYTHMS WOVE THEIR STUPENDOUS CHANT
TO WHICH LIFE STRIVES TO FIT OUR THYME-BEATS
HERE, MELTING OUR LIMITS IN THE ILLIMITABLE,
TUNING THE FINITE TO INFINITY.

- SRI AUROBINDO GHOSE

A SEA OF POSSIBILITIES

DO THE FISH IN THE OCEAN
SEE ALL THERE IS TO SEE
ONE JUMPED OUT OF THE WATER
COULD IT POSSIBLY BE

THERE'S ANOTHER DIMENSION
WITH STRANGE CREATURES, LAND AND TREES
I'D BETTER DIVE BACK TO SAFETY
IT'S SCARY OUT OF THE SEA

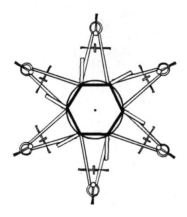

SOUL CONTENT

**RELUCTANCE
TO GO WITHIN
IS FEAR
OF THE CONTENTS
OF THE SOUL**

*TRULY IN THIS WORLD THERE IS NOTHING SO
PURIFYING AS KNOWLEDGE; HE WHO IS PERFECTED IN
YOGA, IN TIME FINDS THIS WITHIN.*
*- BHAGAVAD GITA
CH. 4, VER. 38*

THE QABALA

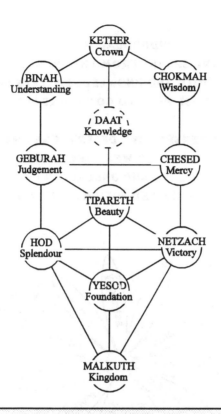

THE SACRED SEFIROT ARE TEN AS ARE THEIR
NUMBERS. THEY ARE THE TEN FINGERS OF THE HANDS,
FIVE CORRESPONDING WITH FIVE. BUT IN THE MIDDLE
THEY ARE KNOTTED UNITY. THERE ARE TEN SEFIROT.
TEN AND NOT NINE; TEN, AND NOT ELEVEN. IF ONE
ACTS AND ATTEMPTS TO UNDERSTAND THIS WISDOM
HE SHALL BECOME WISE. SPECULATE, APPLY YOUR
INTELLIGENCE, AND USE YOUR IMAGINATION
CONTINUALLY WHEN CONSIDERING THEM SO THAT BY
SUCH SEARCHING THE CREATOR MAY BE RE-
ESTABLISHED UPON HIS THRONE.

- SEFIR YETZIRAH

CONTAINER OF LOVE

INDIVIDUAL SOULS
ARE SPARKS FROM THE CREATOR
WHAT TRUTH AND KNOWLEDGE SLEEPS INSIDE
WHOSE PATH TO GOD IS GREATER

ALL PERSPECTIVE DESERVES RESPECT
NO MATTER WHAT THE CHOICE
LET LOVE AND UNDERSTANDING
BE CONTAINED WITHIN EACH VOICE

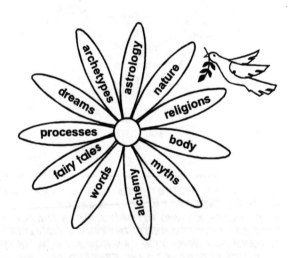

MY TASK IS TO ACCEPT OTHERS, NOT TO APPROVE OF
OTHERS.

- GREG ANDERSON
THE CANCER CONQUEROR

BLUEBIRD

THE BEAUTY OF THE UNIVERSE
RESIDES INSIDE OF ME
EVEN IN MY DREAMS AT NIGHT
THE WONDER THAT I SEE

LAST NIGHT I SAW A BLUEBIRD
GENTLY FLY IN FRONT OF ME
AS I SAT SHARING WITH MY SISTER
UNDERNEATH A WILLOW TREE

MOTHER NATURE HAS THE ANGELS TELL THE BIRDS TO
GO CHECK ON THE HUMANS TO MAKE SURE THEY ARE
OKAY. THE BIRDS TELL THE ANGELS IF WE ARE IN
DANGER. THAT'S WHY BIRDS FLY OVER YOUR CAR AND
WHY YOU SEE BIRDS EVERYWHERE.
— ORIANNE THOMPKINS
(AGE 5)
ANGEL WISDOM

THE LABYRINTH

THE VIBRANCY OF COLOR
DANCING
IN A FIELD
OF QUEEN ANNE'S LACE

SUPPORTING
A SILENT JOURNEY
TO THE CENTER

AT NIGHT,
THE LIGHT
REFLECTING SOULS
THERE TO PARTAKE
OF THEMSELVES

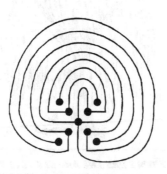

POOR INTRICATED SOUL! RIDDLING, PERPLEXED,
LABYRINTHICAL SOUL!

JOHN DONNE
(1572-1631)
(ENGLISH POET)

BE CAREFUL WHAT YOU PRAY FOR

HAVE YOU EVER ASKED FOR GUIDANCE
WHEN YOU'RE FEELING STRESSED
AND SWEAR THAT WHEN IT COMES
YOU'LL CONSIDER YOURSELF BLESSED

THEN LIKE MAGIC COMES THE ANSWER
EVEN SOONER THAN YOU HOPED
BUT, BECAUSE IT CAME SO QUICKLY
IT WAS DIFFICULT TO COPE

"BE CAREFUL WHAT YOU PRAY FOR"
I'M SURE YOU'VE HEARD BEFORE
YOU CAN MANIFEST YOUR HOPES AND DREAMS
ON THE WINGS OF TRUST YOU'LL SOAR

MISSED OPPORTUNITY
LEAVES ON THE FIRST TRAIN OUT OF TOWN
IN SEARCH OF A MAN WITH COURAGE
AND A PLACE WITH NO LOST AND FOUND

DIGGING A LOT OF SHALLOW HOLES WILL NEVER GET
YOU A WELL.
                                    - RAMAKRISHNA

AS ABOVE, SO BELOW

WE WONDER WHY ALIEN RACES
HAVE TECHNOLOGY THAT WE CAN'T MATCH
HOW MUCH CAN MAN ACCOMPLISH
WHEN HE HAS TO START OVER FROM SCRATCH

MAYBE THESE ALIEN BEINGS
LEARNED A LONG TIME AGO
A CONCEPT WE'VE YET TO MASTER
AS ABOVE, SO BELOW

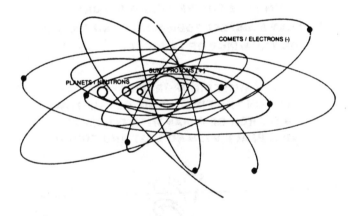

GOD IS THE SHEPHERD, HUMANS ARE THE SHEEP, AND
THE STAR PEOPLE ARE THE SHEEP DOGS.
- LEO SPRINKLE
WHEN COSMIC CULTURES MEET CONFERENCE,
MAY 1995 WASHINGTON, D.C.

THE SEARCH

WE SEARCH WITHIN
AND SPREAD OUR WINGS
DISCOVER FREEDOM
AND THE POWER OF KINGS

OUR ANGELIC ESSENCE
BORN OF LOVE AND STRIFE
CREATES BEAUTIFUL MUSIC
FOR OUR DANCE OF LIFE

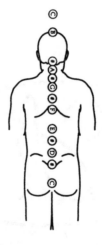

HUMAN MUSIC IS THE HARMONY WHICH MAY BE KNOWN
BY ANY PERSON WHO TURNS TO CONTEMPLATION OF
HIMSELF...IT IS THIS THAT JOIN TOGETHER THE PARTS
OF THE SOUL, AND KEEPS THE RATIONAL PART UNITED
WITH THE IRRATIONAL.

— GIOSEFFE ZARLINO
(1517-1590)
(ITALIAN COMPOSER AND MUSICAL THEORIST)

FRANKINCENSE AND PURR

DO OTHERS FIND CATS REGAL
MYSTERY ILLUMINATES THEIR EYES
INTRIGUING ANTICS FILL THE LIVES
OF BANDIT, ABBEY AND TY

ANCIENT WISDOM LIVES WITHIN
THEY'RE GLAD THAT THEY AREN'T MUTTS
COULD THEIR PREVIOUS OWNERS HAVE BEEN
AKHENATON, CLEO AND TUT

DOGS COME WHEN THEY ARE CALLED; CATS TAKE A MESSAGE AND GET BACK TO YOU.
-MARY BLY

SOUL FOOD

TEARS AND LAUGHTER
ARE FOOD FOR THE SOUL
THEY CLEANSE OUR HEARTS
HELP MAKE US WHOLE

PLANT SEEDS OF PEACE
FOR PAST MISTAKES
AND HARVEST JOY
INSTEAD OF HEARTACHE

THE CENTRAL SECRET IS, THEREFORE, TO KNOW THAT
THE VARIOUS HUMAN PASSIONS AND FEELINGS AND
EMOTIONS IN THE HUMAN HEART ARE NOT WRONG IN
THEMSELVES, ONLY THEY HAVE TO BE CAREFULLY
CONTROLLED AND GIVEN A HIGHER AND HIGHER
DIRECTION, UNTIL THEY ATTAIN THE VERY HIGHEST
CONDITION OF EXCELLENCE.

VIVEKANANDA
(1863-1902)
(INDIAN RELIGIOUS LEADER AND TEACHER)

SIMPLE LESSONS

SOME LESSONS ARE SO SIMPLISTIC
AS THE PAIN OF LIFE WE BEAR
FOR INSTANCE WHEN WE BUMP OUR HEAD
IT'S JUST A REMINDER TO BE MORE AWARE

THINGS TURN OUT BEST FOR PEOPLE WHO MAKE THE
BEST OF THE WAY THINGS TURN OUT.
                                    - ART LINKLETTER

WHO DONE IT

REINCARNATION HAS MUCH IN COMMON
WITH A GOOD MYSTERY BOOK
RETURNING AGAIN AND AGAIN
WITH A NEW PERSPECTIVE WE LOOK

WILL WE FIND A NEW PIECE OF THE PUZZLE,
LEARN WHAT WE'RE HERE TO DO
OR ONCE MORE PERUSE THE FIRST CHAPTER
FINDING OUT WE'RE STILL ON PAGE TWO

DISCOVERING RELEVANT ANSWERS
BY ASKING HOW, WHEN AND WHY
WE APPROACH THE END OF THE BOOK
DETECTING WHO DONE IT WAS I

THE GREAT WHEEL OF LIFE HAS MANY SPOKES AND
EACH OF US WILL STAND ON EVERY SPOKE AT ONE
TIME OR ANOTHER. THE LESSONS WE LEARN ON EACH
SPOKE BRING US CLOSER TO WHOLENESS AND
HARMONY. DISDAIN FOR THOSE WHO HAVE NOT
LEARNED THESE LESSONS WILL NOT SERVE IN
BRINGING HARMONY.
- JAMIE SAMS
THE SACRED PATH CARDS

IS THE TADPOLE HAPPIER BEING A FROG

DEATH   OFF
BIRTH   ON

SLEEP   SPIRIT
AWAKE   MATTER

WINTER   DARK
SPRING   LIGHT

NIGHT   FINISH
DAY   START

CATERPILLAR   TRANSFORMATION
BUTTERFLY   REINCARNATION

TADPOLE   UNSEEN
FROG   SEEN

PAST   END
PRESENT   BEGIN

SILENT   DEATH
SOUND   BIRTH

THE MIRACLE IS THAT THE UNIVERSE CREATED A PART
OF ITSELF TO STUDY THE REST OF IT, AND THAT THIS
PART IN STUDYING ITSELF FINDS THE REST OF THE
UNIVERSE IN ITS OWN NATURAL INNER REALITIES.

- JOHN C. LILLY

THOUGHTS

OUTER NEGATIVITY
ORIGINATES
FROM WITHIN,
PROMPTING
REGURGITATION
FROM OVER INDULGENCE
IN NEGATIVE PERCEPTION,
NEGATIVE THOUGHTS

TRUST
THAT YOU DESERVE
JOY
AND WONDER

SOAR
ON THE WINGS OF CHOICE,
PLEASANTLY SURPRISED
AT YOUR POWERS
OF MANIFESTATION

CHANGE YOUR THOUGHTS,
CHANGE YOUR WORLD

THOUGHTS ARE LIKE BOOMERANGS.
- EILEEN CADDY
THE DAWN OF CHANGE

EARTH ANGEL

SPECIAL FRIENDS ENRICH OUR LIFE
AN ANGEL'S WINGS GRACE MARY ELLEN
WHERE DISCOVERY WILL LEAD US NEXT
THERE'S NO EARTHLY WAY OF TELLIN'

IMAGINATION CELEBRATES
ADVENTURE'S JOURNEY SO FAR
POSSIBILITY MOTIVATES
TWO COMPUTER CHIPS FROM A DISTANT STAR

CONNECTED THROUGH CLOSE FAMILY TIES
BY A BOND OF AUNT AND NIECE
UNIQUENESS EMBODIES
AN ANGELIC ESSENCE OF LOVE AND PEACE

SOME PEOPLE COME INTO OUR LIVES AND QUIETLY
GO. OTHERS STAY FOR A WHILE AND LEAVE
FOOTPRINTS ON OUR HEARTS AND WE ARE NEVER THE
SAME.
- LORRAINE ORTNER-BLAKE
ARTIST

PRISONER OF THE MIND

**HOW CAN WE JUSTIFY
MEMORIES OF OTHER TIMES
MAYBE WHEN WE EVOLVE
PAST THE CONFINES OF OUR MIND**

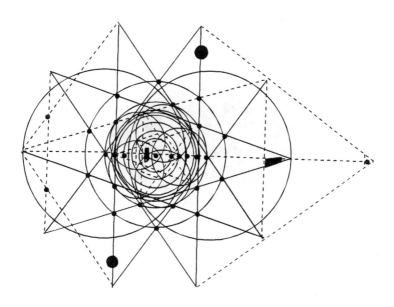

FOR THOSE WHO BELIEVE, NO PROOF IS NECESSARY.
FOR THOSE WHO DON'T, NO PROOF IS POSSIBLE.

- JOHN & LYN ST. CLAIR THOMAS
EYES OF THE BEHOLDER

GARDEN OF EDEN

I ENJOY A CHILDLIKE WONDER
AT THE SPLENDOR OF OUR EARTH
INTRIGUED BY EVERY LIFE FORM
THAT OUR MOTHER CHOSE TO BIRTH

ONE THING TO KEEP IN MIND
IN THIS BEAUTIFUL GARDEN OF EDEN
MAN'S FUTURE JOY DEPENDS UPON
THE CARE WE TAKE WHEN WEEDIN'

THE GREATEST SERVICE TO ANY COUNTRY IS TO ADD A
USEFUL PLANT TO ITS CULTURE.
- THOMAS JEFFERSON

FIREFLY

OUT IN AN OPEN, GRASSY FIELD
A FIREFLY SHINING BRIGHT
ILLUMINATES AS ONE LONE FLASH
A BEACON IN THE NIGHT

OTHERS SEE THE FLICKER
AND JOIN THIS DANCE OF FLIGHT
CREATING IN THE MEADOW
A SYMPHONY OF LIGHT

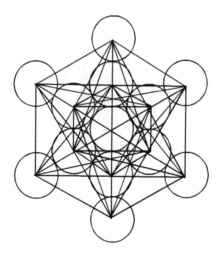

THOSE WHO ARE WISE WILL SHINE LIKE THE
BRIGHTNESS OF THE HEAVENS...LIKE THE STARS FOR
EVER AND EVER.

- DANIEL 12:3

KNOW THYSELF

PLATO WROTE "MAN KNOW THYSELF"
WHAT DO YOU THINK HE MEANT
THAT WE SHOULD LOOK EXTERNALLY
FOR SUBTLE LITTLE HINTS

OR DID HE MEAN TO LOOK INSIDE
ACCESSING ALL WE SEE
TAKING EACH OPPORTUNITY
TO BE THE BEST THAT WE CAN BE

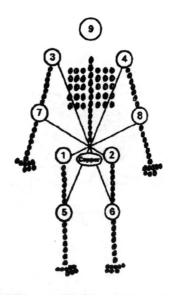

HE WHO KNOWS OTHERS IS WISE, BUT HE WHO KNOWS
HIMSELF IS ENLIGHTENED.
                                    - LAO-TZU

UNITY

I HAD A DREAM
WE'RE AWAKE AND AWARE
FULL OF LOVE AND COMPASSION
WE'VE ALL LEARNED TO CARE

WE'RE A GLOBAL SOCIETY
ALL CONCERNED FOR OUR EARTH
IN AN ATMOSPHERE OF PEACE
WE'VE SURVIVED OUR RE-BIRTH

I AM WIDE-EYED WITH WONDER
WHAT HAVE WE DONE
THEN MY HEART SINGS THE ANSWER
WE ARE UNITY, WE ARE ONE

A NEW WORLD IS ONLY A NEW MIND.
- WILLIAM CARLOS WILLIAMS

ON LOAN

CREATURES OF EARTH SO BEAUTIFULLY UNIQUE
SURROUND OUR GLOBAL SPACES
ARE ANIMALS, PLANTS, EVEN MAN
ON LOAN FROM DISTANT PLACES

*BEFORE THE PHENOMENA OF NATURE, IT IS NECESSARY
TO OBSERVE, TO STUDY AND TO BE ASTONISHED AT
NOTHING.*
- LEIBNITZ

WELL CONNECTED

OUR WORTH IS NOT
WHAT OTHERS THINK
RATHER HOW WE UTILIZE
OUR CONNECTING LINK

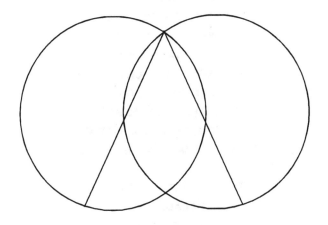

TO FIND YOURSELF, THINK FOR YOURSELF.
- SOCRATES

WHY

WE QUESTION
GOD
CONSTANTLY ASKING
WHY

WHY CHILDREN DIE VIOLENTLY
WHY WAR
WHY PREJUDICE
WHY HUNGER
WHY HOMELESS
WHY CRUELTY TO ANIMALS
WHY POLLUTION
WHY IGNORANCE
WHY MISUSE OF TECHNOLOGY
WHY INEQUALITY
WHY ABUSE OF POWER
WHY OUR PLANET IS DYING
WHY FEAR INSTEAD OF LOVE

THESE CONDITIONS EXIST
BECAUSE OF
ACCEPTANCE
AND
NON-ACCEPTANCE

BECAUSE OF
CHOICE

BECAUSE
WE HAVE MADE
ILLUSION REALITY
AND
REALITY ILLUSION

BECAUSE
WE DON'T MAKE DECISIONS
BASED ON
GREATER GOOD

MAYBE GOD HAS A QUESTION TOO

WHY
DO YOU
ALLOW IT

THERE ARE MANY YOUNG GIRLS, BOAT PEOPLE, WHO
ARE RAPED BY SEA PIRATES... IN MY MEDITATION I
SAW THAT IF I HAD BEEN BORN IN THE VILLAGE OF
THE PIRATE AND RAISED IN THE SAME CONDITIONS AS
HE WAS, THERE IS A GREAT LIKELIHOOD THAT I
WOULD BECOME A PIRATE...IF YOU TAKE A GUN AND
SHOOT THE PIRATE, YOU SHOOT ALL OF US, BECAUSE
ALL OF US ARE TO SOME EXTENT RESPONSIBLE FOR
THIS STATE OF AFFAIRS.

THICH NHAT HANH
PEACE IS EVERY STEP

FEAR NOT

I'M TRYING HARD TO UNDERSTAND
WHERE ALL MY FEAR COMES FROM
AS I SLOWLY CHANGE EACH CELL TO LOVE
I LIKE WHO I'VE BECOME

AS MY CONSCIOUSNESS AWAKENS
I'M SURROUNDED BY SUCH LIGHT
I SWEAR THIS IS THE LAST TIME
I'LL GIVE IN TO UNKNOWN FRIGHT

VICTORY BELONGS TO THE MOST PERSEVERING.

- NAPOLEON

AN OCEAN OF TEARS

THINK OF WHAT WE'RE DOING
TO OUR LIFE FORMS IN THE SEA
CAN YOU HEAR THEM CRY
PLEASE HELP ME

DOLPHINS, WHALES AND MANATEES
ARE EARTH'S KEEPERS OF THE DEEP
AS THEIR HOME BECOMES A DUMPING GROUND
SWIMMING IN SEWAGE, THEY WEEP

IN THE END, IT HARDLY MATTERS WHETHER STAGS, BEAVERS, SEALS, OR ELEPHANTS WEEP. TEARS ARE NOT GRIEF, BUT TOKENS OF GRIEF...A SEAL SURELY FEELS SAD WHEN ITS PUP IS KILLED, WHETHER IT IS DRY-EYED OR NOT. JUST AS A PSYCHIATRIST CANNOT REALLY KNOW WHEN A PERSON HAS CROSSED THE BORDER OF "NORMAL" GRIEF TO "PATHOLOGICAL" MOURNING, SO HUMANS CANNOT KNOW THAT THE WORLD OF SORROW IS BEYOND THE EMOTIONAL CAPACITIES OF ANY ANIMAL.
- FROM "WHEN ELEPHANTS WEEP"

WHEN ONE SEES ETERNITY IN THINGS THAT PASS AWAY, THEN ONE HAS PURE KNOWLEDGE.
- BHAGAVAD GITA

TWO EMOTIONS

LIFE IS PRETTY SIMPLE
THERE ARE ONLY TWO GEARS
IF WE AREN'T LIVING THE EMOTION OF LOVE
WE'VE CHOSEN THE ONE CALLED FEAR

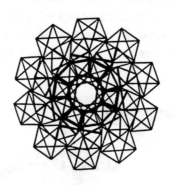

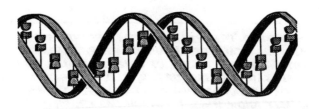

SPIRITUALITY IS NOT TO BE LEARNED BY FLIGHT FROM
THE WORLD, BY RUNNING AWAY FROM THINGS, OR BY
TURNING SOLITARY AND GOING APART FROM THE
WORLD. RATHER, WE MUST LEARN TO PENETRATE
THINGS AND FIND GOD HERE.
                              - MEISTER ECKHART

SECURITY BLANKET

WHICH MODE OF SECURITY
DO YOU CHOOSE
A RICHLY FURNISHED MANSION,
A BOTTLE OF BOOZE

A PADDED WALLET,
A LAYER OF FAT,
A TWELVE HOUR A DAY JOB,
CHASING YOUR TAIL LIKE A CAT

A BIG EGO,
AN EVEN BIGGER CIGAR,
A BEAUTIFUL ARMPIECE
IN A NEW LUXURY CAR

HAVE YOU EVER WONDERED
SHOULDN'T THERE BE MORE
WELL, THE RAINBOW CONNECTION
IS BEHIND THE THIRD DOOR

EVEN THE FINEST CLOTHES TURN TO RAGS.
-I CHING WISDOM

LIFE'S TOO SHORT

SUBTLE CHANGES
MAKE US SEE
THE LIMITLESS POTENTIAL
TO JUST BE

DON'T PUT LIFE
INTO A BOX
FREE YOUR MIND
UNLOCK THE LOCKS

STOP WORRYING ABOUT
WHAT OTHERS THINK
LIFE'S TOO SHORT
IT'S OVER IN A BLINK

PLAYING WITH CLAY

AFTER YEARS OF GETTING "A'S" IN SCHOOL
I GOT A "D" IN ART
FOR THE NEXT 35 YEARS
I CLOSED MY CREATIVE HEART

AT 46 I TOOK A CHANCE
IN A CLASS WORKING WITH CLAY
LEAVING EXPECTATION AND CONTROL BEHIND
I RECAPTURED MY ABILITY TO PLAY

PERSONAL ART SHOULD NOT BE JUDGED
OR EVER GIVEN A GRADE
THEY'RE UNIQUE EXPRESSIONS OF THE SOUL
I EVEN RECOGNIZED WHAT I MADE

WE DON'T REALIZE IN HOW MANY WAYS
OTHERS EXERT CONTROL
HOW MIGHT HAVE OUR LIVES BEEN DIFFERENT
IF WE HADN'T STOPPED SHORT OF THE GOAL

THE AIM OF ART IS TO REPRESENT NOT THE OUTWARD
APPEARANCE OF THINGS, BUT THEIR INWARD
SIGNIFICANCE.

- ARISTOTLE

BY EXAMPLE

HELPING OTHER'S AWAKEN TO WHAT'S INSIDE
WITHOUT SETTING UP A BOOTH
IS EASIEST DONE IN THE SIMPLEST WAY
BY LIVING OUR OWN TRUTH

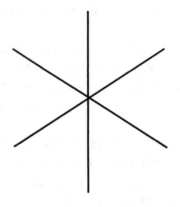

I BELIEVE THAT SPIRITUALITY LIVES FIRST IN ONE'S PERSONAL EXPRESSION OF TRUTH, SECOND, IN THE CHOICE TO FIND COMPANIONSHIP WITH OTHERS, AND THIRD IN THE COURAGE AND SELF DISCIPLINE TO WALK ONE'S TALK IN THE NEXT "FIRE" OR DIMENSION OF EXISTENCE.

— RAINBOW EAGLE

NO LOITERING

NO TIME TO DAWDLE ON THE PATH
DO NOT CRITICIZE OR JUDGE
JUST CONCENTRATE UPON YOURSELF
EMBRACE SPIRIT'S GENTLE NUDGE

MEDITATE DAILY AND GO WITHIN
WHERE THE LIGHT YOU HAVE INSIDE
MEETS THE SILENCE OF YOUR EVERY BREATH
WHERE THE GIFTS OF SOUL ABIDE

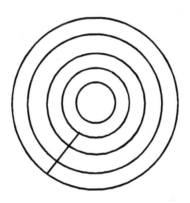

WHEN WE ARE PERFECTED IN TRUTH, ALL ACTS AND
THEIR FRUITS DESCEND UPON US.
— PATANJALI
FROM YOGA SUTRAS OF PATANJALI
BY CHARLES JOHNSTON

OBE

WHOOSHING SOUNDS FROM NOWHERE
ENVELOP MY WHOLE BEING
TRAPPED BY FEAR AND SUDDENNESS
MY MIND TRIES FLEEING

ELECTRICAL SENSATIONS
ENGULFED IN NEEDLES AND PINS
RETURNING HOURS LATER
I WONDER, WHERE HAVE I BEEN

FINALLY RECOGNIZING LOVE
AFTER YEARS OF TURNS AND TOSSES
INTEGRATING HIDDEN FEAR
IS PART OF THE PROCESS

THERE IS ANOTHER WORLD. IT IS HIDDEN IN THIS ONE.
- ANONYMOUS

SOLITUDE

PYRAMIDS AND DOLPHINS,
HEALING, STONES AND ANCIENT LANDS
ARE JUST A FEW LOVES EXPLORED
TURNING PAGES WITH MY HANDS

ABSORBING FAVORITE TOPICS
LIVING EVERY MOMENT IN JOY
IS JUST AS GOOD A FEELING
AS BEING A KID WITH NEW TOYS

THE GIFT OF SPENDING LEISURE TIME
IN PEACEFUL SOLITUDE
WITH CANDLES, BOOKS AND MUSIC
TO SERVE AS SOUL FOOD

CREATES THE PERFECT ATMOSPHERE
TO TEMPT AN OCCASIONAL POEM
I FEEL LIKE THE LUCKIEST PERSON ALIVE
THESE TIMES AT HOME ALONE

FOR OFT, WHEN ON MY COUCH I LIE
IN VACANT OR IN PENSIVE MOOD
THEY FLASH UPON THAT INWARD EYE
WHICH IS THE BLISS OF SOLITUDE
AND THEN MY HEART WITH PLEASURE FILLS
AND DANCES WITH THE DAFFODILS.

- WILLIAM WORDSWORTH

THE BATTLE WITH SELF

EACH DAY IS SUCH A CHALLENGE
FREEING CHOICES LOCKED IN TIME
WILL PEACE AND LOVE AND HAPPINESS
OR GRIEF AND STRIFE BE MINE

THE CALL IS MINE AND MINE ALONE
WHAT WILL THE ANSWER BE
IT CLEARLY LIES WITHIN MY GRASP
I OWN MY DESTINY

THERE IS ONLY ONE SUCCESS, TO BE ABLE TO SPEND
LIFE IN YOUR OWN WAY.
— CHRISTOPHER MORLEY

STRETCH MARKS

LET OUR MINDS BECOME ELASTIC
AND STRETCH THE COMFORT ZONE
NEW OPPORTUNITIES UNVEIL THEMSELVES
AS WE CHALLENGE WHAT IS KNOWN

EXPANSION OF OUR CONSCIOUSNESS
IN ONENESS WE BELONG
AWARENESS WILL HELP US SEE
WHAT HAS BEEN THERE ALL ALONG

MEN MUST BE AWARE OF THE WISDOM AND THE
STRENGTH THAT IS IN THEM IF THEIR UNDERSTANDING
IS TO BE EXPANDED.

VAUVENARGUES
(1715-1747)
(FRENCH SOLDIER, MORALIST)

IN LAK'ECH

THE MAYA HAVE A SAYING
"I AM ANOTHER YOU"
WE'RE EACH AN IMPORTANT INGREDIENT
ALL PART OF THE SAME STEW

THERE ARE CARROTS, ONIONS, POTATOES,
THE FIRE, THE POT, THE KNIFE
THE "FLAVOR" OF ALL ACKNOWLEDGED
VARIETY IS THE SPICE OF LIFE

WINKING AT DESTINY

LIFE IS NOT A DRESS REHEARSAL
OPENING NIGHT WAS THE DAY WE WERE BORN
ENJOY THE BIRTH OF EACH MOMENT
AND IN DEATH WE WON'T HAVE TO MOURN

THERE'S PEACE IN RETURNING TO SPIRIT
IN DEATH WE FINALLY SEE
THE ILLUSION OF FEAR WAS ONLY A TEST
WHILE WINKING AT DESTINY

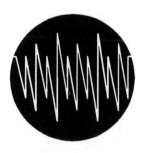

WHEN CONDITIONS ARE NO LONGER SUFFICIENT AND THE FLOWER CEASES TO MANIFEST, WE SAY THE FLOWER HAS DIED, BUT THAT IS NOT CORRECT EITHER.   ITS   CONSTITUENTS   HAVE   MERELY TRANSFORMED THEMSELVES INTO OTHER ELEMENTS, LIKE COMPOST AND SOIL. WE HAVE TO TRANSCEND NOTIONS LIKE BIRTH, DEATH, BEING AND NON-BEING. REALITY IS FREE FROM ALL NOTIONS.
                              - THICH NHAT HANH
            FROM LIVING BUDDHA, LIVING CHRIST

UPS AND DOWNS

WE MISS THE WONDER THAT'S UP
BY ONLY LOOKING DOWN
ADVENTURE ALSO LIVES BEHIND US
WHEN WE TURN AROUND

THE BEAUTY OF A SUNSET
IS SEATED IN THE WEST
MAGIC APPEARS EVERYWHERE
WHEN WE PASS THE OBSERVANCE TEST

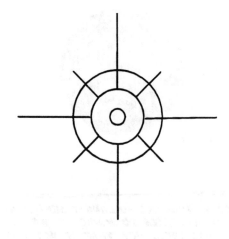

NATURE WILL REVEAL ITSELF IF WE WILL ONLY LOOK.
- THOMAS ALVA EDISON
(1847-1941)
(AMERICAN INVENTOR)

THE TRIP OF A LIFETIME

THE PATH INTO CONSCIOUSNESS
IS THE TRIP OF A LIFETIME
SHORTCUTS DON'T COUNT
ON THIS OUT -OF-BREATH CLIMB

LIBERATION ARRANGED
ONE LAST PARTY FOR FEAR
LAST SEEN WAVING GOODBYE
TO THE FACE IN THE MIRROR

HE WHO HAS BEGUN HIS TASK HAS HALF DONE IT.
- HORACE

BOUNDARY OF REALITY

A LEAP IN EVOLUTION
IS HAPPENING RIGHT NOW
OUR BOUNDARIES OF REALITY
ARE EXPANDING, *AND HOW*

OUR NATURAL EXPERIENCES ARE LIKE PENCILED LINES ON FLAT PAPER. IF OUR NATURAL EXPERIENCES VANISH IN THE RISEN LIFE, THEY WILL VANISH ONLY AS PENCIL LINES VANISH FROM THE REAL LANDSCAPE: NOT AS A CANDLE FLAME THAT IS PUT OUT, BUT AS A CANDLE FLAME WHICH BECOMES INVISIBLE BECAUSE SOMEONE HAS PULLED UP THE BLIND, THROWN OPEN THE SHUTTERS, AND LET IN THE BLAZE OF THE RISEN SUN.

- C. S. LEWIS

STATE OF GRACE

THE SEED OF GRACE WAS PLANTED
WITHIN US LONG AGO
WITH LOVE AND LIGHT WE'VE WATERED
AND WATCHED OUR GARDEN GROW

A PERENNIAL WORTH HAVING
IS MORE THAN JUST A STATE
THIS PRICELESS GIFT OF ELEGANCE
CAN RID THE WORLD OF HATE

ANGER AND HATRED ARE THE MATERIALS FROM
WHICH HELL IS MADE.

— THICH NHAT HANH

EVICTION NOTICE

**OUR PLANET WILL SURVIVE
BY THE POWER OF CONVICTION
OR MOTHER EARTH WILL SERVE
HER NOTICE OF EVICTION**

THE CHESS BOARD IS THE WORLD, THE PIECES ARE
THE PHENOMENA OF THE UNIVERSE, THE RULES OF
THE GAME ARE WHAT WE CALL THE LAWS OF NATURE.
THE PLAYER ON THE OTHER SIDE IS HIDDEN FROM US.
WE KNOW THAT HIS PLAY IS FAIR, JUST, AND PATIENT.
BUT ALSO WE KNOW, TO OUR COST, THAT HE NEVER
OVERLOOKS A MISTAKE, OR MAKES THE SMALLEST
ALLOWANCE FOR IGNORANCE.
                                    - THOMAS HENRY HUXLEY

SILVER LINING

HUMBLE BEGINNINGS
ARE A PLUS
YOU GROW UP
ALREADY THINKING US

EXPAND THIS VIRTUE
TO THE WHOLE
ITS STRENGTH
LINES THE MEDICINE BOWL

TRUTH IS SO EXCELLENT, THAT IF IT PRAISES BUT SMALL THINGS THEY BECOME NOBLE.
- LEONARDO DA VINCI

THE LAW OF ATTRACTION

WHEN I LIKE ME
SO DO OTHERS
STRANGERS, FRIENDS,
SISTERS, BROTHERS

AS I REMEMBER
LIKE ATTRACTS LIKE
IT WILL BE NO SURPRISE
IF PEOPLE TAKE A HIKE

IF YOU NEGLECT YOUR GOOD QUALITIES AND VIRTUES,
YOU WILL CEASE TO BE OF VALUE TO YOUR FRIENDS
AND NEIGHBORS. SOON, NO ONE WILL SEEK YOU OUT
OR BOTHER ABOUT YOU.
                                    - I CHING WISDOM

THE BEST MEDICINE

HAVE YOU EVER LAUGHED SO LONG AND HARD
THAT YOU COULDN'T STOP WHEN YOU TRIED
THEN, JUST WHEN THINGS WERE UNDER CONTROL
YOU BEGAN LAUGHING AGAIN TILL YOU CRIED

THIS HAPPENED ON A TRIP WITH FRIENDS
WHO KNOWS WHAT CAME OVER US THAT DAY
IF I WERE A BETTING PERSON
THERE WAS HEALING THROUGH HUMOR I'D SAY

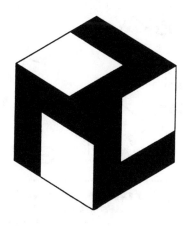

EVERY ONCE IN A WHILE, SILLINESS JUST MIGHT BE
NEXT TO GODLINESS.
                              -ANGEL WISDOM

CANCER ANSWER

THERE'S TRUTH IN ALL RELIGIONS
NOT ONE HAS ALL THE ANSWERS
FIGHTING TO SEE WHO IS RIGHT
HAS CAUSED A WORLD FULL OF CANCER

IF I COULD MAKE ONE CHANGE
WE'D STOP MIMICKING ATILLA THE HUN
AND WITH COMPASSION AND UNDERSTANDING
GREET EACH OTHER WITH HUGS, NOT GUNS

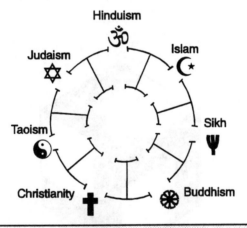

WHEN YOU ARE A TRULY HAPPY CHRISTIAN, YOU ARE
ALSO A BUDDHIST. AND VICE VERSA.
                                    - THICH NHAT HANH

YOU BECOME A CANCER CONQUEROR NOT BECAUSE
YOU GO INTO REMISSION - INSTEAD, YOU BECOME A
CANCER CONQUEROR BECAUSE YOU CHOOSE TO
BECOME A NEW PERSON.
                                    - GREG ANDERSON
                                    THE CANCER CONQUEROR

A DAMSEL IN FULL DRESS

OUT ON A LIMB SAT A DAMSEL FLY
WATCHING WITH GREAT INTENT
AS A WOMAN TENDED HER GARDEN
BOTH CASUALLY CAME AND WENT

THEY VIEWED EACH OTHER IN SILENCE
THEIR IRIDESCENCE REFLECTING THE SUN
TREADING LIGHTLY, A BOND WAS FORMED
AS ENERGIES MERGED INTO ONE

APPRISED OF HER BEAUTY
DAMSEL ACKNOWLEDGED THE GARDENER'S TOO
SOON TRUST BECAME THE CATALYST
THAT UNIFIED THIS COUP

THE WOMAN WAS GRANTED PERMISSION TO TOUCH
SHE GENTLY STROKED THE FACE
A TEAR ERUPTED FROM DEEP INSIDE
THERE WAS JOY ALL OVER THE PLACE

DAMSEL'S EYES GREW WIDE WITH INTEREST
AT THE ATTEMPT OF ONE MORE THING
DRAWING THE LINE AT SURVIVAL
SHE TOOK LEAVE AS A HAND BRUSHED HER WINGS

DOTH NOT NATURE ITSELF TEACH YOU?
- I CORINTHIANS 11:14

MAYAN TEACHER

SIMPLE PLEASURES GREET HIS DAY,
A SINGING SHELL, A SOARING HAWK
A SIMPLE SAYING GREETS HIS FRIENDS
XATA ZAC XATA AMAC

ON OCCASION, A MAYAN TIMEKEEPER
COMES TO OUR AREA TO TEACH
CLIMBING THE TREE OF KNOWLEDGE
NO BRANCH IS BEYOND OUR REACH

WE'VE EXPLORED TOGETHER A PLACE WITHIN
THAT SHELTERS WISDOM AND POWER
SHARING GIFTS OF BEAUTY WITH NATURE
WHERE TIME DOES NOT LIVE IN THE HOUR

A LOVING CONNECTION TO MAN AND EARTH
AND OUR ANCESTORS FROM THE STARS
IS EXPERIENCED IN VARIOUS LOCATIONS
ONLY PART OF THE JOURNEY'S BY CAR

HIS TIMELY PASSING THROUGH MY LIFE
MAKES THIS SIMPLE FACT QUITE CLEAR
IT'S TRUE THAT WHEN THE STUDENT IS READY
THE TEACHER WILL APPEAR

THERE ARE SOME SECRETS WHICH DO NOT PERMIT
THEMSELVES TO BE TOLD.
                              - EDGAR ALLEN POE
                     FROM "THE MAN IN THE CROWD"

III

BALANCE BEAM

SOMETIMES I CHOOSE TO ACHIEVE BALANCE
STANDING QUIETLY ON ONE FOOT

WHY NOT USE BOTH FEET
AND MAKE LIFE EASIER

I LIKE A CHALLENGE

BEGIN DIFFICULT THINGS WHILE THEY ARE EASY. DO
GREAT THINGS WHEN THEY ARE SMALL. THE
DIFFICULT THINGS OF THE WORLD MUST ONCE HAVE
BEEN EASY; THE GREAT THINGS MUST HAVE BEEN
SMALL...A THOUSAND MILE JOURNEY BEGINS WITH ONE
STEP.

- LAO-TZU

SENSITIVITY TRAINING

IMAGINE BEING CAPTURED
AND PUT IN A TINY CAGE
HAS MAN BECOME DESENSITIZED
CAN HIS CONSCIOUSNESS BE RAISED

WOULD YOU LIKE FEEDING YOUR CHILD,
DOING YOUR DUTY IN PLAIN VIEW,
HAVING YOUR FAMILY TORN APART
LIKE THOSE LIVING IN A ZOO

HOW ABOUT SWIMMING IN CIRCLES
OR JUMPING THROUGH HOOPS ALL DAY
AND THEN BEING REWARDED
WITH ROTTEN FISH AS PAY

FREEDOM FOR ALL IS IMPORTANT
LIFE SHOULD NOT LIVE BEHIND BARS
OUR FEAR IS NOT OF THE UNKNOWN
WE FEAR WHAT WE ALREADY ARE

THE INDIAN ELEPHANT IS SAID SOMETIMES TO WEEP.
- CHARLES DARWIN

COMMON SCENTS

LIFE STINKS ON OCCASION
WHEN TROUBLES REFUSE TO FIND A CURE
EFFORT AND TIME PRODUCE ROSES
THE MOST BEAUTIFUL GROW IN MANURE

TO JUDGE YOU BY YOUR FAILURES IS TO CAST BLAME
UPON THE SEASONS FOR THEIR INCONSTANCY.

- KAHLIL GIBRAN
THE PROPHET

OPEN MINDED

EXPANSION OF OUR CONSCIOUSNESS
IS REALLY NOTHING NEW
AS WE'VE GROWN THROUGH THE AGES
WE'VE REVISED HOW, WHEN AND WHO

WE'RE AT THE MERCY OF OUR MIND
AND WHAT IT KNOWS RIGHT NOW
OUR PERCEPTION OF REALITY
CAN CHANGE IN A MOMENT TO "WOW"

GOD HAS SAID, "THERE ARE SEVENTY THOUSAND VEILS
BETWEEN YOU AND ME. BUT THERE ARE NO VEILS
BETWEEN ME AND YOU."
— SHEIKH MUZAFFER OZAK

ANTENNA FOR GOD

HE IS A CHILD OF THE UNIVERSE
AN ANTENNA FOR GOD
A PEACEMAKER
A MAN ONE WITH ALL
A WISE MAN
A MAN OF LOVE

A MAN WHO LIVES THE MYSTERY
AND WALKS IN TRUTH
COURAGE
STRENGTH
INTEGRITY
BEAUTY
AND COMPASSION

WHO IS PURE OF HEART
UNDERSTANDING
NON-JUDGMENTAL
GRACIOUS
OPEN MINDED
APPROACHABLE
INTUITIVE
HUMEROUS
KIND
FORGIVING
SINCERE
HUMBLE
TRUSTING

HE IS RAINBOW EAGLE
PEACE SHIELD TEACHER
FRIEND
AGAIN

I BELIEVE THAT A FIFTH REASON FOR THE RE-
EMERGENCE OF NATIVE PHILOSOPHY IS THAT IT IS
TIME FOR ALL PEOPLE TO SHARE THEIR TRUTHS AND
DEVELOP OUR "RELATEDNESS" AS PLANET EARTH
WALKERS. THIS IS THE SPECIFIC PURPOSE OF THE
PEACE SHIELD.

- RAINBOW EAGLE
SEVENTH FIRE
PEACE SHIELD TEACHER

PERCEPTION

HOW MANY BEAUTIFUL MOMENTS
CAN YOU COUNT AT THE END OF THE DAY
DID YOU CAPTURE ALL THE BEAUTY
OF LIFE'S GIFTS THAT CAME YOUR WAY

THE FLOWERS AND BIRDS, THE SUN AND MOON
THE STILLNESS OF A BROOK
A WAGGING TAIL, A CHILD'S BRIGHT SMILE
THE GREAT ENDING OF A BOOK

A GENTLE HUG, A QUIET NAP,
A FRIEND'S CALL TO SAY HELLO
AN UNEXPECTED REFUND CHECK
WE'RE MORE FORTUNATE THAN WE KNOW

THE NEXT TIME THAT YOU'RE FEELING DOWN
CHANGE YOUR STATE OF MIND AND SEE
THAT BLESSINGS COME IN BIG AND SMALL
PERCEPTION IS THE KEY

THE WAY TO REDUCE THE PAIN WHICH YOU ASSOCIATE
WITH EARTHLY EXPERIENCES AND EVENTS - BOTH
YOURS AND THOSE OF OTHERS - IS TO CHANGE THE
WAY YOU BEHOLD THEM.

- NEAL DONALD WALSCH
CONVERSATIONS WITH GOD
BOOK I

LONE TEAR

WHAT HAVE WE DONE WITH TECHNOLOGY
HAVE WE USED IT FOR GREATER GOOD
OR EXPLOITED THE PEOPLE OF EARTH
AND TAKEN WHENEVER WE COULD

NATIVE AMERICANS HONOR THE LAND
AND RESPECT MOTHER EARTH'S PLACES
THEY LOOK WITH SADNESS AT WHAT WE'VE DONE
CAN YOU SEE THE LONE TEAR ON THEIR FACES

WE HAVE NOT INHERITED THE EARTH FROM OUR
FATHERS, WE ARE BORROWING IT FROM OUR
CHILDREN.
                          - NATIVE AMERICAN SAYING

TOO MANY CHIEFS

**WOULD WE ALLOW
THESE INSENSITIVE LOGOS
FOR OTHER
AMERICAN SPORTS TEAMS**

**CHIEF WHOPOO
ITALIAN AMERICAN**

**CHIEF MICKOO
IRISH AMERICAN**

**CHIEF CHICKEEPOO
WOMEN'S TEAM NAME**

**CHIEF CHINKOO
ASIAN AMERICAN**

**CHIEF KIKEOO
JEWISH AMERICAN**

**CHIEF POLLOCKOO
POLISH AMERICAN**

**CHIEF SAMBOO
AFRICAN AMERICAN**

**CHIEF SPICKOO
LATIN AMERICAN**

WHO WILL PROTEST
UNDIGNIFIED PORTRAYALS
OF NATIVE AMERICANS,
OF CHIEF WAHOO,
OF CHANTING IMPOSTORS
FEIGNING TOMAHAWKS

HAVE WE BECOME
SO BLINDED BY APATHY,
SO ABSORBED IN OUR OWN WORLD
THAT WE FAIL TO RECOGNIZE
THE VOICE OF DESPAIR IN OTHERS

WILL WE CONTINUE
TO SHOUT
OUR SILENT ACCEPTANCE
OF UNJUSTNESS
OR TAKE A STAND
FOR INTEGRITY AND FAIRNESS

HOW MUCH LONGER
BEFORE
RESPECT FOR ALL RACES,
THE HUMAN RACE,
IS AS IMPORTANT
AS EGO,
POWER AND MONEY

CAN'T WE HONOR
THE SIMPLE REQUEST
OF THOSE WHO'VE BEEN HERE LONGER
THAN ALL OF THE REST

ALL THAT IS IN TUNE WITH THEE, O UNIVERSE, IS IN
TUNE WITH ME!
                                    - MARCUS AURELIUS

OPRAH

THE WORLD COULD USE MORE OPRAH'S
A HUMAN BEING WHOSE HEART
IS FULL OF LOVE FOR MANKIND
AND PERFECTLY CAST IN HER PART

A TRUE HUMANITARIAN
WHO COULD HAVE USED HER FAME
FOR STRICTLY SELFISH REASONS
INSTEAD SHE RAISED HER AIM

SHE SET HER SIGHT ON PROGRAMS
TO HELP US EASE OUR PAIN
AS PEOPLE LEARN TO HEAL THEMSELVES
SHE KNOWS THAT SHE TOO GAINS

WINNING MANY UPHILL BATTLES
SOME RIGHT IN OUR OWN HOMES
HEAVEN KNOWS SHE AT LEAST DESERVES
TO HAVE A POEM OF HER OWN

HUMOROUS, FRIENDLY, DOWN TO EARTH
SHE SHINES WITH PURE INTENT
WHEN ALL IS SAID AND DONE
ONE WOMAN *HAS* MADE A DIFFERENCE

SOMETIMES OUR LIGHT GOES OUT, BUT IT IS BLOWN
INTO FLAME BY AN ENCOUNTER WITH ANOTHER HUMAN
BEING. EACH OF US OWES THE DEEPEST THANKS TO
THOSE WHO HAVE REKINDLED THIS INNER LIGHT.

- ALBERT SCHWEITZER

WHY WAIT

I'M OPEN TO
CHANGING
MY MIND
TOMORROW

BASED
ON
NEW EXPERIENCES
TODAY

IT'S THE ONLY
THING
I KNOW
FOR SURE

I MIGHT
NOT
EVEN WAIT
UNTIL TOMORROW

FACTS DO NOT CEASE TO EXIST BECAUSE THEY ARE
IGNORED.
- ALDOUS HUXLEY

LIGHTEN UP

LIVING IN LOVE
REQUIRES
AN OPEN MIND,
OPEN EYES,
AND OPEN HEART

NOT NECESSARILY
IN THAT ORDER

LIGHTEN UP

... BE DARING, BE FEARLESS, AND DON'T BE AFRAID
THAT SOMEBODY IS GOING TO CRITICIZE YOU OR
LAUGH AT YOU. IF YOUR EGO IS NOT INVOLVED, NO
ONE CAN HURT YOU.

— GURU R.H.H.

ABUNDANCE
ACCEPTANCE
ADVENTURE
BALANCE
BEAUTY
BROTHERHOOD
CHARITY
CLARITY
COMPASSION
COURAGE
CREATIVITY
DETACHMENT
DISCERNMENT
EFFICIENCY
ENTHUSIASM
FAITH
FLEXIBILITY
FORGIVENESS
FREEDOM
GRACE
GRATITUDE
HARMONY
HEALING
HONESTY
HOPE
HUMOR
INSPIRATION

CONGRATULATIONS

BEFORE ENLIGHTENMENT CHOPPING WOOD AND CARRYING WATER.

DEGREE

WISDOM
WILLINGNESS
UNDERSTANDING
TRUTH
TRUST
TENDERNESS
SYNTHESIS
SURRENDER
STRENGTH
SPONTANEITY
SIMPLICITY
SILENCE
RESPONSIBILITY
PURPOSE
PROSPERITY
POWER
PLAY
PEACE
PATIENCE
OPENNESS
OBEDIENCE
LOVE
LIGHT
KNOWLEDGE
JOY
INTEGRITY
INTEGRATION
ON YOUR MASTER'S DEGREE!!!

AFTER ENLIGHTENMENT CHOPPING WOOD AND CARRYING WATER.

- ZEN PROVERB

SILENCE SPEAKS

SPEAKING VOLUMES
SILENCE HOLDS ITS BREATH
ANTICIPATING
AN UNOBSTRUCTED JOURNEY
TO THE CENTER

EXPRESSIONS OF WISDOM
EXPLODE
CREATING WAVES OF ECSTASY
SEIZING AGAIN
THE LIMITS OF JOY

AS ABOVE, SO BELOW.
- THE EMERALD TABLET OF HERMES TRISMEGISTUS

NO COMPETITION

SATISFIED, THE PUZZLE WAITS
TO SOLVE ITSELF AS TIME ALLOWS
THEN, COMPETITION REARS ITS HEAD
EGO'S ON THE PROWL

A FLAG FALLS AT THE STARTING GATE
ON YOUR MARK, GET SET, GO
NO BATTLE FOR THIS FINISH LINE
THE RACER IS ALONE

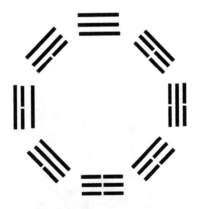

THE I CHING DOES NOT OFFER ITSELF WITH PROOFS
AND RESULTS; IT DOES NOT VAUNT ITSELF, NOR IS IT
EASY TO APPROACH. LIKE A PART OF NATURE, IT
WAITS UNTIL IT IS DISCOVERED.
                                    - CARL JUNG

ADVENTURE OF A LIFETIME

LIFE'S PATH IS LIKE AN ATLAS
NO TWO JOURNEYS ARE THE SAME
SOME CHOOSE THE STRAIGHT AND NARROW
FOR OTHERS THAT'S TOO TAME

TRYING TO GET FROM HERE TO THERE
IS EVERYBODY'S GOAL
IF YOU'RE LUCKY YOU CAN MAKE THE TRIP
PAYING ONLY A FEW TOLLS

TAKE TIME TO SMELL THE FLOWERS
WHILE ENJOYING ALL THE SIGHTS
AND DURING THIS ADVENTURE
MAY ALL YOUR LIGHTS BE WHITE

LIFE IS EITHER A DARING ADVENTURE OR NOTHING.
                              - HELEN KELLER

THE CLOCK WITHOUT A FACE

IF WE LEARN TO LIVE IN THE PRESENT
TOMORROW WILL NEVER APPEAR
INTEGRATE LOVE AND COMPASSION
AND THERE'LL BE NO ROOM FOR FEAR

TIME IS BORN OF ILLUSION
A TWIN TO THE ENERGY OF SPACE
CAPTURE THE POWER OF THE MOMENT
NOW NOTICE, THE CLOCK HAS NO FACE

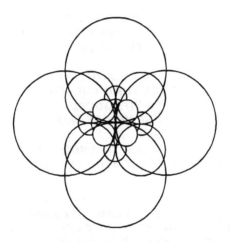

IN AN INSTANT, RISE FROM TIME AND SPACE. SET THE
WORLD ASIDE AND BECOME A WORLD WITHIN
YOURSELF.

- SHABESTARI
(C. 1250-1320)
(PERSIAN SUFI POET)

EVOLUTION

MAN WILL NOT BE SAVED
AT THE EXPENSE
OF THE OTHER LIFEFORMS
ON THIS PLANET

AS A GUARDIAN,
HE HAS FAILED

HIGHER FORMS OF HUMANITY
ARE BEING CREATED
TO CO-EXIST IN HARMONY
WITH NATURE

THEY WILL REALIZE
THEIR CONNECTION
TO ALL OF LIFE

GENETIC MANIPULATION
IS THE FORM CHOSEN
TO INTRODUCE
THESE NEW BEINGS

THIS PROCESS OF EVOLUTION
IS NOT A NEWLY USED TECHNIQUE

ANIMALS ARE, LIKE US, ENDANGERED SPECIES ON AN
ENDANGERED PLANET, AND WE ARE THE ONES WHO
ARE ENDANGERING THEM, IT, AND OURSELVES. THEY
ARE INNOCENT SUFFERERS IN A HELL OF OUR
MAKING...WHEN ANIMALS ARE NO LONGER COLONIZED
AND APPROPRIATED BY US, WE CAN REACH OUT TO
OUR EVOLUTIONARY COUSINS. PERHAPS THEN THE
ANCIENT HOPE FOR A DEEPER EMOTIONAL
CONNECTION ACROSS THE SPECIES BARRIER, FOR
CLOSENESS AND PARTICIPATION IN A REALM OF
FEELINGS NOW BEYOND OUR IMAGINATION, WILL BE
REALIZED.

- FROM "WHEN ELEPHANTS WEEP"

THE BUCK STOPS HERE

LEISURELY STROLLING A WINDING TRAIL
A BUCK, A DOE AND A FAWN
ENJOYING THE PEACEFUL SOLITUDE
IT'S SLIGHTLY AFTER DAWN

A CLICK RUPTURES THE SILENCE
THE HERD RAISES ITS HEAD
A HUNTER'S PRAYER IS ANSWERED
WITH A THUNDEROUS BANG, BUCK'S DEAD

FOR MYSELF, I HAVE NOT EVER BEEN ABLE WITHOUT
DISTRESS TO SEE PURSUED AND KILLED AN INNOCENT
ANIMAL WHICH IS DEFENSELESS AND WHICH DOES US
NO HARM. AND AS IT COMMONLY HAPPENS THAT THE
STAG, FEELING HIMSELF OUT OF BREATH AND
STRENGTH, HAVING NO OTHER REMEDY LEFT, THROWS
HIMSELF BACK AND SURRENDERS TO OURSELVES WHO
ARE PURSUING HIM, ASKING FOR OUR MERCY BY HIS
TEARS...THAT HAS ALWAYS SEEMED TO ME A VERY
UNPLEASANT SPECTACLE.

- MONTAIGNE
FROM 1580 ESSAY "OF CRUELTY"

FAMILIAR STRANGERS

ON A RECENT TRIP TO A POWER PLACE
I MET STRANGERS OR SO I THOUGHT
IT DIDN'T TAKE LONG TO DISCOVER
MY CONNECTION TO MOST OF THE LOT

HOW INCREDIBLE TO HAVE MORE IN COMMON
WITH THOSE JUST RECENTLY MET
THAN SOME KNOWN THIS ENTIRE LIFETIME
RENEWED FRIENDSHIP CAN BE A SURE BET

REMEMBERED PAST LIFE ENCOUNTERS
MADE SOME OF US REALIZE
THAT LESSONS AND GOALS ARE INTERTWINED
BY A BOND THAT TIME CAN'T DISGUISE

THERE IS NO MAN ALONE, BECAUSE EVERY MAN IS A
MICROCOSM, AND CARRIES THE WHOLE WORLD ABOUT
HIM.
                                    - SIR THOMAS BROWNE

THE SOUND OF FREEDOM

SOME ARE AFRAID THAT GIFTS FROM SPIRIT
COME FROM AN "EVIL" SOURCE
THEY DON'T UNDERSTAND THAT MAN'S PSYCHIC ABILITY
IS A POWERFUL, LOVING FORCE

MANY WOULD RATHER SURRENDER THEIR STRENGTHS
AND BE TOLD WHAT TO DO
BY AUTHORITY FIGURES WHO LOVE THEIR JOB
OF CONTROLLING THE MASSES, *THAT'S YOU*

BE RESPONSIBLE FOR YOUR OWN ACTIONS
THERE'S SUCH FREEDOM IN THIS CHOICE
YOU'LL NEVER TURN OVER YOUR POWER AGAIN
ONCE YOU RECOGNIZE YOUR OWN VOICE

*OH, THE DIFFICULTY OF FIXING THE ATTENTION OF
MEN ON THE WORLD WITHIN THEM!*

*SAMUAL TAYLOR COLERIDGE
(1772-1834)
(ENGLISH POET AND CRITIC)*

DYING TO PLEASE

I WAS SAD TO READ
IN THE PAPER TODAY
A 14 YEAR OLD BOY
LOST HIS BATTLE TO STAY

HE WAS DIFFERENT,
SENSITIVE, QUIET AND SHY
AND DIDN'T FIT IN,
THOUGH HE FERVENTLY TRIED

DO WE LACK THE COMPASSION
AND TOLERANCE TO SEE
THAT OTHERS ARE LITERALLY
DYING TO PLEASE

WHY MUST WE FEAR
WHEN WE DON'T UNDERSTAND
WILL OUR HEARTS REMAIN CLOSED
TO OUR FELLOWMAN

UNLESS WE BECOME
ACCEPTING OF OTHERS
COMMITTING TO LIVE
AS SISTERS AND BROTHERS

WE'LL EVENTUALLY
LACK DIVERSITY
WHEN WE LOOK IN THE MIRROR,
GUESS WHAT WE'LL SEE

GONE IS A WONDERFUL SON,
BROTHER AND FRIEND
WHOSE SPIRIT IS FREE NOW,
NO NEED TO PRETEND

THIS STRANGER WAS DEEPLY
TOUCHED BY YOUR PAIN
AND PRAYS TO GOD
THAT YOUR DEATH'S NOT IN VAIN

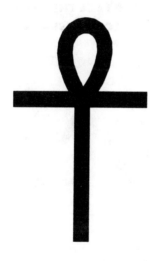

THE REAL VOYAGE OF DISCOVERY CONSISTS NOT IN
SEEKING NEW LANDS BUT SEEING WITH NEW EYES.

MARCEL PROUST
(1871-1922, FRENCH NOVELIST)

THE SUMMIT

WE DO NOT
REACH THE SUMMIT
BY WISHING...
AS WE ACKNOWLEDGE
EACH STEP,
EACH STUMBLE
WE BEHOLD
THE CREATION
OF OUR UNIVERSE
AND FEEL THE JOY
OF ACCOMPLISHMENT

THOSE WHO CONSIDER THEIR PATH SUPERIOR ARE
CONDESCENDING. A PARROT WHO SPEAKS OF THE
TOTALITY OF THE SELF IS ABSURD. MANY PATHS LEAD
TO THE SUMMIT, BUT IT TAKES A WHOLE BODY TO GET
THERE.

- 365 TAO
BY DENG MING-DAO

THE ILLUSION OF FEAR

WHY IS REINCARNATION
SO HARD TO COMPREHEND
EACH SPRING NATURE REVEALS
LIFE AGAIN AND AGAIN

WHAT SEEMED TO DIE IN WINTER
WAS JUST WAITING TO REAPPEAR
FROM THIS CYCLE OF LIFE IS BORN
THE GRAND ILLUSION OF FEAR

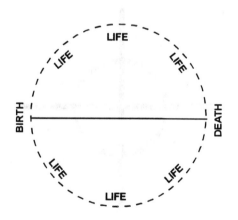

A LITTLE WHILE, A MOMENT OF REST UPON THE WIND,
AND ANOTHER WOMAN SHALL BEAR ME.
— KAHLIL GIBRAN
THE PROPHET

THE SEARCH

IN SEARCH OF SELF, WE GO WITHIN
TO FIND LIFE'S SOLUTIONS
WHEREIN LIES THE SECRETS
OF HUMAN EVOLUTION

UNFOLD UNTO THE UNIVERSE
RELINQUISH FEAR EACH DAY
AS A MASTER KEY UNLOCKS
TIME RELEASED DNA

EVERYTHING THAT IS WITHIN CAN BE KNOWN BY WHAT
IS WITHOUT.
                                        - PARACELSUS

TAPPING THE SOURCE

IT'S IMPORTANT TO MEDITATE
TWICE A DAY
BUT, I CAN HEAR
THE EXCUSES GALORE

I'VE USED THEM MYSELF,
THE KIDS, I'M TOO TIRED
OR I'M JUST
RUNNING OUT THE DOOR

A FEW MINUTES OF SILENCE
EACH MORNING AND NIGHT
TWO TIMES 20
IS PAR FOR THE COURSE

A SIMPLE TOOL
THAT CAN CHANGE YOUR LIFE
AS YOU TAP
THE UNIVERSAL LIFE FORCE

IMAGINATION IS MORE IMPORTANT THAN KNOWLEDGE.
- ALBERT EINSTEIN

THE PLACE CALLED HELL

WE'RE DOMINATED BY OUTSIDE FORCES
THE MORE WE DEPEND ON THEM
BREAK FREE FROM THIS SELF-IMPOSED PRISON
BY TRUSTING WHAT'S WITHIN

UNDILUTED POTENTIAL
IS CONTAINED WITHIN EACH CELL
UNLEASH LIMITATION OR FIND
THE MIND IS THE PLACE CALLED HELL

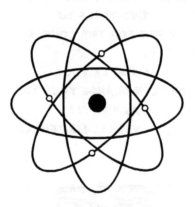

KNOWING YOURSELF IS A TALLER ORDER THAN YOU
THINK.
                                    - ANGEL WISDOM

GREAT EXPECTATIONS

I'VE GOT A TIP FOR HAPPINESS
YOU WON'T BELIEVE WHAT YOU'RE SEEING
JUST DON'T EXPECT PEOPLE TO BE
MORE THAN THEY'RE CAPABLE OF BEING

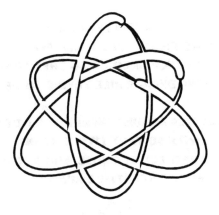

IF YOU JUDGE PEOPLE, YOU HAVE NO TIME TO LOVE
THEM.
                                    - MOTHER TERESA

VOYAGE OF CHAINS

THEY WERE BROUGHT FROM LANDS ACROSS THE SEA
COMPLETELY AGAINST THEIR WILL
UNLIKE THOSE WHO CAME HERE FREELY
FORCED TO SWALLOW A BITTER PILL

INSTEAD OF RESPECTING THEIR CULTURES
WE TOLD THEM WHITE WAS BETTER AND BIGGER
AND WITH VENOM IN OUR VOICES
TO THEIR FACES CALLED THEM NIGGER

OVER 100 YEARS AGO
WE FINALLY SET THEM 'FREE'
THEY RAN UNCHAINED OR SO THEY THOUGHT
MANY DYING WHILE TRYING TO BE

SUCCESS AGAINST INCREDIBLE ODDS
WITH SO VERY LITTLE MEANS
ELICITS RESPECT BY THOSE WHO RECOGNIZE
A RACE OF BEAUTIFUL HUMAN BEINGS

NON-VIOLENCE IS A POWERFUL AND JUST WEAPON. IT
IS A WEAPON UNIQUE IN HISTORY, WHICH CUTS
WITHOUT WOUNDING AND ENNOBLES THE MAN WHO
WIELDS IT. IT IS A SWORD THAT HEALS.
                                    - MARTIN LUTHER KING, JR.

NIGHT VISION

PAY ATTENTION TO YOUR DREAMS
THEY'RE MORE THAN SCARY SIGHTS & SCREAMS
TEACHERS COME IN MANY GUISES
IN THIS WORLD OF WONDER AND SURPRISES

WHEN THE BOUNDARY OF REALITY SLIPS
ROCK THAT BOAT, LET IT TIP
OPEN YOUR MIND, LET IT SOAR
LIGHT CAN'T ENTER A CLOSED DOOR

BELIEVE IT OR NOT, I AWOKE ONE DAY
WITH RANDOM THOUGHTS OF DNA
UNLIMITED VISION STALKS THE NIGHT
WHERE OUR FEARS ARE SURROUNDED BY LIGHT

ALL WE SEE OR SEEM IS BUT A DREAM, WITHIN A DREAM.
                                        - EDGAR ALLEN POE

PERSONAL MEDICINE

MEDICINE BUNDLE
CONTAINER OF STRENGTH
SHARED BY AND WITH
ALL OF CREATION

A FEATHER, A STONE
COUNTLESS TOTEM FRIENDS
ARRIVE UNANNOUNCED
RANDOM GIFTS FROM SPIRIT

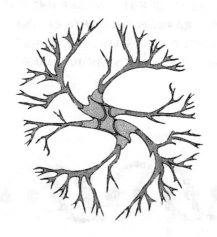

TREE AT MY WINDOW, WINDOW TREE, MY SASH IS
LOWERED WHEN NIGHT COMES ON; BUT LET THERE
NEVER BE CURTAIN DRAWN BETWEEN YOU AND ME.

- ROBERT FROST

FEAR

FEAR IS A WAY OF KEEPING US FROM WORKING WITH ENERGY THAT WE ARE NOT YET READY TO WORK WITH

OUR DOUBTS ARE TRAITORS, AND MAKE US LOSE THE GOOD WE OFT MIGHT WIN BY FEARING TO ATTEMPT.

- WILLIAM SHAKESPEARE

THE GIFT OF TOLERANCE

THERE ARE CERTAIN TRAITS YOU ARE BORN WITH
AND OTHERS THAT ARE ACQUIRED
SEXUAL PREFERENCE JUST HAPPENS
TO DEPEND ON HOW YOU ARE WIRED

BEING STRAIGHT OR GAY IS NOT A CHOICE
CHEMICAL MAKE-UP IS PART OF YOUR HEALTH
BE TOLERANT OF THOSE WHO ARE DIFFERENT FROM YOU
IT'S A GIFT YOU GIVE TO YOURSELF

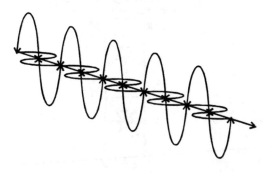

PERFECT KINDNESS ACTS WITHOUT THINKING OF
KINDNESS.
                                        - LAO-TZU

GOOD GOD

IN SEARCHING FOR TRUTH
I'VE COME TO KNOW
THAT GOD IS SO GOOD
SHE ONLY NEEDS ONE "O"

DON'T BRISTLE
AT WHAT YOU SEE
THE FEMININE ASPECT
ALSO CONTAINS HE

THE WHOLE LIGHT - GOD, TRUTH - IS BEYOND OUR
PERCEIVING. GOD IS VEILED. SOME PEOPLE HAVE
TROUBLE BELIEVING IN A GOD WHO LOOKS INTO ANY
EYES BUT THEIRS. OTHERS HAVE TROUBLE BELIEVING
IN A GOD THEY CANNOT SEE. BUT THAT NONE OF US
CAN LOOK DIRECTLY INTO GOD'S EYES CERTAINLY
DOESN'T MEAN THAT GOD ISN'T THERE, MYSTERIOUS,
UNKNOWABLE, GAZING INTO OURS.

- F. FORRESTER CHURCH,
ENTERTAINING ANGELS

SECRETS

WHAT SECRETS DO THE PYRAMIDS HOLD
IS ANCIENT WISDOM STORED IN STONE
ARE THEY MERELY CHAMBERS FOR LONG AGO KINGS
JUST A PLACE TO REST THEIR BONES

WHAT ABOUT STONEHENGE AND EASTER ISLAND
OTHER MYSTERIES EXPLORED DOWN THRU THE AGES
WHY HAVEN'T THESE SILENT RELICS OF NATURE
REVEALED ANSWERS TO EVEN OUR GREATEST SAGES

WE SIT AROUND IN A CIRCLE AND SUPPOSE, AND THE
SECRET SITS IN THE MIDDLE AND KNOWS.

- ROBERT FROST

HOW BIZARRE

WHEN THEY VISIT FROM OTHER DIMENSIONS
OR COME FROM ANOTHER STAR
WILL WE GREET THEM WITH LOVE NO MATTER WHAT
HOW BIZARRE IS TOO BIZARRE

LOVING ENERGY FROM OTHER REALMS
EXISTS AT THE END OF OUR TEARS
WHAT KEEPS US FROM CONSCIOUS CONTACT
IS THE POWER OF OUR FEARS

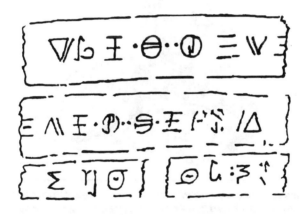

FOR THE WORLD IS NOT PAINTED OR ADORNED, BUT
IS FROM THE BEGINNING BEAUTIFUL; AND GOD HAS
NOT MADE SOME BEAUTIFUL THINGS, BUT BEAUTY IS
THE CREATOR OF THE UNIVERSE.

— RALPH WALDO EMERSON

RAINBOW BRIDGE

IN HEAVEN THERE'S A RAINBOW BRIDGE
BUILT WITH BRILLIANT COLORS
CONNECTED TO PROVIDE SUPPORT
EACH BLENDING WITH THE OTHER

ALL COLORS SHINE WITH PURPOSE
BASKING IN SELF-WORTH
LET MANKIND JOIN TOGETHER
AND CREATE HEAVEN ON EARTH

WHEN YOUR ARE INSPIRED BY SOME GREAT PURPOSE, SOME EXTRAORDINARY PROJECT, ALL YOUR THOUGHTS BREAK THEIR BONDS; YOUR MIND TRANSCENDS LIMITATIONS. YOUR CONSCIOUSNESS EXPANDS IN EVERY DIRECTION, AND YOU FIND YOURSELF IN A NEW, GREAT AND WONDERFUL WORLD. DORMANT FORCES, FACULTIES, TALENTS BECOME ALIVE, AND YOU DISCOVER YOURSELF TO BE A GREATER PERSON BY FAR THAN YOU EVER DREAMED YOURSELF TO BE.

— PATANJALI

THE IMPORTANCE OF ONE

**THE PEARL WAS BIRTHED
BY A GRAIN OF SAND
SMALL GESTURES COUNT
LEND A HELPING HAND**

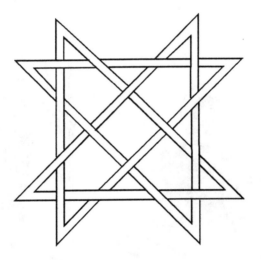

OUT OF THE ONE COMES TWO; OUT OF THE TWO COMES
THREE; AND OUT OF THE THREE COME THE TEN
THOUSAND THINGS.
                                    - THE TAO TEH CHING

KUAN YIN - HATHOR - MARY

THE BENEVOLENCE OF NATURAL LAW LIES IN ASSURING US THAT...MIRACLES ARE OPEN TO US, BUT IT DOES NOT EXTEND TO TELLING US HOW TO ACCOMPLISH THEM; IT IS FOR US TO DISCOVER THE KEYS, THE ENCODINGS AND DECODINGS BY WHICH THEY CAN BE BROUGHT TO PASS.

- ROBERT ROSEN
THEORETICAL BIOLOGIST

THE HARP

WISDOM OF THE SEA

WHAT'S HIDDEN WITHIN OUR OCEANS
CIVILIZATIONS OF THE PAST
ARE ABORIGINAL SECRETS
BURIED IN THESE TOMBS SO VAST

RELICS MEANT TO SURVIVE
GIVE CLUES TO SOME OF LIFE'S MYSTERIES
MEXICO, EGYPT, HAWAII, PERU
CONTAIN REMNANTS OF OUR EARLY HISTORY

WHEN COUNTRIES FINALLY STOP WARRING
CHANGING CONCERN FROM "ME" TO "WE"
MAN CAN EXPLORE ANCIENT KNOWLEDGE
AT THE BOTTOM OF THE SEA

NATURE IS WRITTEN IN SYMBOLS AND SIGNS.

- JOHN GREENLEAF WHITTIER
(1807-1892, AMERICAN POET)

WHAT A COINCIDENCE

SACREDNESS LIVES EVERYWHERE
AWAKENED EYES NOW SEE
DID I FIND SYNCHRONICITY
OR IT DISCOVER ME

LIVING IN THE WORLD WITHOUT INSIGHT INTO THE
HIDDEN LAWS OF NATURE IS LIKE NOT KNOWING THE
LANGUAGE OF THE COUNTRY IN WHICH ONE WAS BORN.

- HAZRAT INAYAT KHAN
(1882-1927)
(SUFI SPIRITUAL GUIDE, MUSICIAN, AND WRITER)

THE FAN

RECOGNIZING
OTHER STATES OF VIBRATION
IS LIKE LOOKING
AT A FAN

WHEN IT'S STILL,
ALL BLADES
ARE CLEARLY
VISIBLE

LOW SPEED
APPEARS LESS SOLID,
MEDIUM
EVEN LESS

HUMMING ON HIGH,
THE BLADES
ARE BLURRED
TO THE NAKED EYE

THROUGHOUT
THE DANCE OF FLUCTUATION
IT REMAINS
A FAN

ARE YOU
ANY MORE FEARFUL
OF IT ON HIGH
THAN TURNED OFF

OR
DO YOU ACCEPT ALL OF
THE FAN'S CAPABILITIES
AS NATURAL

YOU AND THE FAN
HAVE MUCH IN COMMON
ACCEPT YOURSELF,
ACCEPT OTHERS

THE SNOW GOOSE NEED NOT BATHE TO MAKE ITSELF WHITE. NEITHER NEED YOU DO ANYTHING BUT BE YOURSELF.

- LAO-TZU

JOY, JOY

**CREATE MOMENTS OF JOY
IN ALL THAT YOU DO
WITH A SENSE OF WONDER
EVERYTHING IS NEW**

THE ACTION OF THE CHILD INVENTING A NEW GAME
WITH HIS PLAYMATES; EINSTEIN FORMULATING A
THEORY OF RELATIVITY; THE HOUSEWIFE DEVISING A
NEW SAUCE FOR THE MEAT; A YOUNG AUTHOR WRITING
HIS FIRST NOVEL; ALL THESE ARE IN TERMS OF
DEFINITION, CREATIVE, AND THERE IS NO ATTEMPT TO
SET THEM IN SOME ORDER OF MORE OR LESS
CREATIVE.

— CARL R.ROGERS

TRUE ESSENCE

PRESENTED IN THE DREAM STATE
GLOWING BALLS OF LIGHT
REACHING OUT, ACCEPTING
GOLDEN EMBERS BURNING BRIGHT

WHAT DOES IT REPRESENT
IS IT KNOWLEDGE THAT I'M SEEING
OR THE CORE OF MY TRUE ESSENCE
AN ETERNAL LIGHT BEING

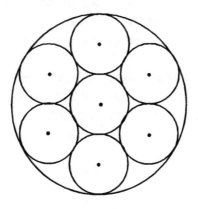

GEOMETRY IS KNOWLEDGE OF THE ETERNALLY
EXISTENT.

- PLATO

THE VILLAGE CHILD

CAN YOU FEEL THE PAIN
AN ABUSED CHILD'S CRY
SCREAMS GO UNREPORTED
CHILDHOOD SENSELESSLY DIES

CAN PARENTS BE PROTECTORS
WHEN THERE'S ANGER STORED WITHIN
TO CALLOUSLY HARM OUR CHILDREN
IS THE WORLD'S VILEST SIN

PHYSICAL HURTS SCAR THE BODY
A PASSING WINCE OF DISDAIN
EMOTIONAL TRAUMA SCARS THE HEART
CAN YOU FEEL THE PAIN

ABUSE CANNOT GO UNNOTICED
GET INVOLVED WHEN YOU SEE SOMEONE RILED
BECOME PART OF THE AFRICAN SAYING
IT TAKES A WHOLE VILLAGE TO RAISE A CHILD

YOUR CHILDREN ARE NOT YOUR CHILDREN, THEY
COME THROUGH YOU BUT NOT FROM YOU...FOR THEIR
SOULS DWELL IN THE HOUSE OF TOMORROW, WHICH
YOU CANNOT VISIT, NOT EVEN IN YOUR DREAMS.
                                    - KAHLIL GIBRAN
                                        THE PROPHET

ONE STEP PROGRAM

SELF-LOVE IS IMPORTANT
A MANDATORY TOOL
THE FIRST STEP TOWARD ACCEPTANCE OF ALL
AS DESCRIBED IN THE GOLDEN RULE

THOSE WHO DO WHAT THEY LOVE ARE IN TUNE WITH THEIR PURPOSES ON EARTH.
- ANGEL WISDOM

THE STORY TELLER

THE STORY TELLER CAME TO SHARE
THE MAGIC OF HER SELF
MANY SPECIAL TREASURES SHE REVEALED
WITH THE ENCHANTMENT OF AN ELF

WE LAUGHED AND CRIED, UNVEILED OUR TRUTH
OUR TONGUES AND TAILS WERE WAGGIN'
USING ALL GOD'S CREATURES GREAT AND SMALL
EVEN RALPH THE MYTHICAL DRAGON

A LOVING BOND WAS FORMED THAT NIGHT
THERE WAS TRUST AMONG THE CRONES
WE'LL FOREVER REMEMBER THE PARTS WE PLAYED
THIS GROUP OF WOMEN KNOWN AS "CIRCLE OF STONES"

ALWAYS WE HOPE SOMEONE ELSE HAS THE ANSWER.
SOME OTHER PLACE WILL BE BETTER. SOME OTHER
TIME IT WILL ALL TURN OUT. THIS IS IT. NO ONE ELSE
HAS THE ANSWER. NO OTHER PLACE WILL BE BETTER,
AND IT HAS ALREADY TURNED OUT.
                                                    - LAO-TZU

SOUL POSSESSION

**WHAT DO WE REALLY OWN IN LIFE
THAT HELPS US PLAY OUR ROLE
IN THE END WE DON'T OWN ANYTHING
MORE IMPORTANT THAN OUR SOUL**

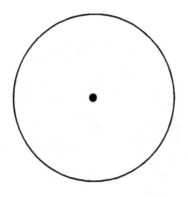

IN MY END IS MY BEGINNING.

*MOTTO OF MARY,
QUEEN OF SCOTS
(1542-1587)*

SPIRALING TOWARD ETERNITY

SPIRALING TOWARD ETERNITY
DESTINED TO MEET AGAIN
REMEMBERED ANCIENT VIBRATIONS
REUNITED IN LOVE AS FRIENDS

WHERE HAVE YOU JOURNEYED SINCE LAST WE MET
YOUR PRESENCE BRINGS MEMORIES OF HOME
DO YOU ALSO OFTEN MISS
THE CITY OF LIGHTS AND CRYSTAL DOMES

I BELIEVE THE GEOMETRIC PROPORTION SERVED THE
CREATOR AS AN IDEA WHEN HE INTRODUCED THE
CONTINUOUS GENERATION OF SIMILAR OBJECTS FROM
SIMILAR OBJECTS.

- JOHANNES KEPLER
(1571-1630, GERMAN ASTRONOMER)

I REMEMBER WHEN

SWEEPING THOUGHTS OF LONG AGO
WANDER THROUGH MY MIND
LIKE PEACEFUL SCENES ON CANVAS
THEY REFLECT ANOTHER TIME

GRASSES SWAYING GENTLY
SOFT WINDS BRAID THE HAIR
SINCERE REGARD FOR NATURE
SWEET FRESHNESS FILLS THE AIR

CONTRAST PAINTS THE LANDSCAPE
CONNECTING NOW TO THEN
ARCHIVES FLOOD THE MEMORY
AS I REMEMBER WHEN

MAKE IT SO THAT TIME IS A CIRCLE AND NOT A LINE.
- SIMONE WEIL

COSMIC ORIGIN

**IN THE U. S.
WE'RE ALL AMERICANS
WITH OUR HERITAGE
SCATTERED ALL OVER THE EARTH**

**HAVE YOU EVER THOUGHT
OF YOUR COSMIC HOME
DO YOU KNOW
YOUR UNIVERSAL ORIGIN OF BIRTH**

WHEN THE PSYCHICAL NATURE TAKES ON THE FORM OF
THE SPIRITUAL INTELLIGENCE, BY REFLECTING IT,
THEN THE SELF BECOMES CONSCIOUS OF ITS OWN
SPIRITUAL INTELLIGENCE.

— PATANJALI

SERVING LIFE

HOW LONG UNTIL ASCENSION
SINCE NOBODY KNOWS
LET'S NOT WASTE TIME WONDERING
WHEN IT'S TIME TO GO

MAKE THE CHOICE TO SERVE LIFE
AS FULLY AS YOU CAN
LIKE ONE TWO THOUSAND YEARS AGO
AN EXTRAORDINARY MAN

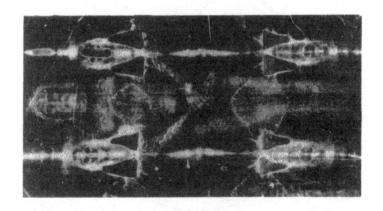

HE THAT BELIEVES ON ME, THE WORKS THAT I DO HE
SHALL DO ALSO, AND GREATER WORKS THAN THESE
SHALL HE DO...

- JESUS
JOHN 14:12

GREAT TEACHERS INCARNATE FROM TIME TO TIME TO
TRY TO TEACH MAN TO LOVE HIS NEIGHBOR AND TO
LIVE IN A PEACEFUL, HELPFUL MANNER WITH OTHERS.

- DAVID HATCHER CHILDRESS

THE WORRY STONE

A WORRY STONE BOUGHT FOR MY ROCK COLLECTION
BROKE IN HALF AS I WALKED IN THE DOOR
COULD THAT NOT SO SUBTLE SIGN SUGGEST
SIMPLY NOT TO WORRY ANY MORE

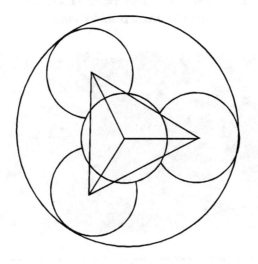

WORRY IS AN ADDICTION THAT INTERFERES WITH
COMPASSION.

— 365 TAO

EARTH CHANGES

EARTH HAS BEEN CHANGING FOR BILLIONS OF YEARS
TRANSFORMATION IS NOTHING NEW
BECAUSE OF CHOICES MADE BY MAN
SHE HAS MAJOR CLEANSING TO DO

WE'LL BE WHERE WE'RE SUPPOSED TO BE
DON'T CONCENTRATE ON FEAR
JUST LISTEN TO YOUR INNER VOICE
AND GET THAT ENGINE IN GEAR

PROTECTING THE PHYSICAL BODY
SHOULD NOT BE OUR ONLY GOAL
MORE IMPORTANT IS THE WORK WE DO
FOR THE SURVIVAL OF OUR SOUL

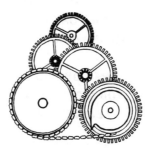

EACH THING IS OF LIKE FORM EVERLASTING AND
COMES ROUND AGAIN IN ITS CYCLE.
- MARCUS AURELIUS

HERKY

A SMALL CHILD CALLS
COME PLAY WITH ME
TO A FRIEND
THAT ONLY SHE CAN SEE

WILL YOU STAY
AND HAVE SOME TEA
IT'S SO EXCITING
BEING THREE

I'D SET A PLACE
FOR YOU TO EAT
LET NO ONE ELSE
SIT IN YOUR SEAT

THEN ONE DAY
YOU WENT AWAY
LEAVING ME
ALONE TO PLAY

I WAS SAD
BUT SOMEHOW KNEW
THAT YOU WOULD ALSO
MISS ME TOO

A NEW EMOTION
BECAME CLEAR
I THINK THE GROWN-UPS
CALLED IT FEAR

YEARS WENT BY
AND I FORGOT
MOST EVERYTHING
THAT I WAS TAUGHT

GUESS TIME WAS NEEDED
ON MY OWN
NOW ONCE AGAIN
I HEAR THE TONES

REMINDING ME
THE TIME IS NOW
TO FINALLY
REMEMBER HOW

TO GATHER
ALL THE LESSONS GAINED
AND SHARE THE GIFTS
BOTH LOVE AND PAIN

EVENTUALLY
I GAVE UP FEAR
AND WELCOMED BACK
WHAT ONCE WAS NEAR

THE CHOICE OF LOVE
IS WONDER-FILLED
REPLACING EGO'S
TEST OF WILL

I KNOW YOU'RE REAL
AND NOT PRETEND
BECAUSE THIS TIME
YOU BROUGHT YOUR FRIENDS

LOVE IS LETTING GO OF FEAR.
- GERALD JAMPOLSKY

THE POWER OF WINGS

DREAMING, TUMBLING, SOARING HIGH
ORBITING A STAR-STUDDED NIGHTTIME SKY
OH MY, A PLANET STREAKED BY

BEAUTIFUL HUES OF PINK, ORANGE RINGS
NO WONDER THE ROBIN SINGS
OH MY, THE POWER OF WINGS

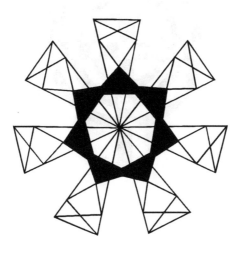

AH, BUT A MAN'S REACH SHOULD EXCEED HIS GRASP,
OR WHAT'S A HEAVEN FOR?
- ROBERT BROWNING

MEMORIES

WHY AM I DRAWN TO MYSTICAL PLACES
MT. SHASTA, MEXICO, HAWAII, PERU
ARE MEMORIES TRIGGERED OF OTHER LANDS
SUCH AS ANCIENT ATLANTIS AND MU

SOMETIMES GOD STRENGTHENS TIMID SOULS WITH
TIMELY REVELATIONS IN ORDER TO KEEP THEM FROM
ALL FEAR AT THE MOMENT OF DEATH.

- GREGORY THE GREAT,
DIALOGUES

CROP CIRCLES

CROP CIRCLES
ARE SOUND FREQUENCIES
EMITTED
TO AWAKEN A RESPONSE
IN DNA

THE BEAUTIFUL IS A MANIFESTATION OF THE SECRET LAWS OF NATURE... WHEN NATURE BEGINS TO REVEAL HER OPEN SECRET TO A PERSON, HE FEELS AN IRRESISTIBLE LONGING FOR HER MOST WORTHY INTERPRETER, ART.
- JOHANN WOLFGANG GOETHE
(1749-1832, GERMAN POET)

FAR OUT

DO NOT FEAR INTELLIGENT LIFE FROM AFAR
IT IS THEY WHO ARE AGHAST
THESE BEINGS WHO VISIT WILL CERTAINLY BE
MORE BENEVOLENT THAN WE'VE BEEN IN THE PAST

THE FAULT, DEAR BRUTUS, LIES NOT IN OUR STARS
BUT IN OURSELVES.
- WILLIAM SHAKESPEARE,
JULIUS CAESAR

BAH BAH

OUR DESTINY IS TO FIND OUR TRUTH
WHATEVER THAT MIGHT BE
LET EACH UNIQUE EXPERIENCE
BECOME A LOCK THAT FINDS ITS KEY

WE'RE NOT ON EARTH TO BE LIKE SHEEP
AND FOLLOW EGOTISTICAL MAN
RELEASE THE FEAR AND DOUBT YOU'VE LEARNED
BELIEVE IT AND YOU CAN

DO NOT GIVE UP YOUR POWER
CHOOSE YOUR INNER STRENGTH TO MEND
KNOW THE LIGHT AND PEACE AND LOVE YOU SEEK
IS JUST AROUND THE BEND

HE REJOICETH MORE OF THAT SHEEP, THAN OF THE
NINETY AND NINE WHICH WENT NOT ASTRAY.

- MATTHEW 18:13

LIGHT WORKER

WE'RE HERE TO BE GOD'S HELPERS
NOT ALWAYS AN EASY TASK
YOU'D THINK WITH ALL THAT LIGHT
HE'D SAY "JUST SIT AROUND AND BASK"

NO TIME FOR THAT, THERE'S WORK TO DO
WE EACH PLAY LEADING PARTS
OUR MOST IMPORTANT ROLE
IS HEALING OUR OWN HEART

CHOOSE ALWAYS THE WAY THAT SEEMS RIGHT,
HOWEVER ROUGH IT MAY BE. PRACTICE WILL MAKE IT
EASY AND PLEASANT.
                              - ATTRIBUTED TO PYTHAGORAS

SETTING SAIL

TO JOURNEY
INTO CONSCIOUSNESS
IS TO SET SAIL
UPON THE BREATH OF GOD

THE MOST BEAUTIFUL THING WE CAN EXPERIENCE IS
THE MYSTERIOUS. IT IS THE SOURCE OF ALL TRUE ART
AND SCIENCE.
                                    - ALBERT EINSTEIN

NIGHT SCHOOL

I HAVE SEEN BROWN WRINKLY SKIN
AND OTHER BEINGS, SOME WOMEN, SOME MEN
ALL SHADES AND SHAPES, BOTH SHORT AND TALL
EVEN THOSE WHO MANIFEST AS AN ENERGY BALL

THEY TEACH ME IN MY DREAMS AT NIGHT
LOVE ALL OF LIFE, RELEASE THE FRIGHT
I'M WORKING HARD TO CONQUER FEAR
AS I SUCCEED, THEY RE-APPEAR

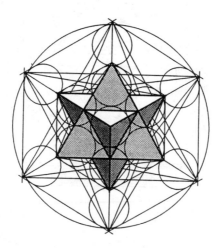

IF YOU WOULD UNDERSTAND THE INVISIBLE, LOOK
CAREFULLY AT THE VISIBLE.
                                        - TALMUD

DISTINCTLY DIFFERENT

EACH EXPERIENCE
MAKES US UNIQUE
TO FIND OUR ANSWERS
WE CONSTANTLY SEEK

LIKE A FINGERPRINT
PERSPECTIVE IS DISTINCT
AS WE HONOR OUR DIFFERENCES
IN ONENESS WE ARE LINKED

A MAN IS THE WHOLE ENCYCLOPEDIA OF FACTS. THE
CREATION OF A THOUSAND FORESTS IS IN ONE ACORN,
AND EGYPT, GREECE, ROME, GAUL, BRITAIN, AMERICA,
LIE FOLDED ALREADY IN THE FIRST MAN.

- RALPH WALDO EMERSON

BATTERY CHARGE

SOMETIMES I FEEL LIKE SOARING
AND MY MIND DECIDES TO GO
TO SPACES FILLED WITH LIGHT
PLACES THAT GOD KNOWS

RETURNING FROM THE JOURNEY
I FIND THE STRENGTH TO START
THE BATTERY OF FLOWING LOVE
CONTAINED WITHIN MY HEART

THE SECRET OF SUCCESS IS MAKING YOUR VOCATION
YOUR VACATION.
                                    - MARK TWAIN

UNIVERSAL AMBASSADOR

OUR PURPOSE IS TO INTEGRATE
THIS PATH OF LIFE WE CHOSE
AND TEACH THAT WHEN WE HEAL OURSELVES
WE LESSEN EARTHLY WOES

A CONSENSUAL AGREEMENT REACHED
LONG BEFORE THIS BIRTH
MAPPED A PATH FOR THE JOURNEY
TO THE BEAUTIFUL PLANET EARTH

MANY LOVING LIFE FORMS
ASSIST US, BELIEVE IT OR NOT
THEY PATIENTLY WATCH OUR COSMIC PLAY
CHANGING SOME OF US THOUGHT BY THOUGHT

WE ARE STAR-STUFF CONTEMPLATING THE STARS.
- CARL SAGAN

LIVING ON THE EDGE

**WHEN WE UNLOCK THE MYSTERIES
HIDDEN WITHIN THE SOUL
WE FIND ANSWERS THAT LIVE
AT THE EDGE OF IMAGINATION**

*IF YOU'RE NOT LIVING ON THE EDGE, YOU'RE TAKING
UP TOO MUCH SPACE.*

*- DR. GARY YOUNG
YOUNG LIVING ESSENTIAL OILS*

KEYS TO THE ATTIC

HOW MANY DIFFERENT LIFE FORMS
DO YOU THINK EXIST OUT THERE
IF IT'S ANY INDICATION
LOOK AT PLANET EARTH TO COMPARE

OPEN UP YOUR MIND AND SEE
JUST STEP OUTSIDE YOUR BOX
A MAJESTIC, WONDROUS WORLD EXISTS
WHEN YOU FINALLY UNLOCK THE LOCKS

THE HARMONY OF THE WORLD IS MADE MANIFEST IN
FORM AND NUMBER, AND THE HEART AND SOUL AND
ALL THE POETRY OF NATURAL PHILOSOPHY ARE
EMBODIED IN THE CONCEPT OF MATHEMATICAL
BEAUTY.
- SIR D'ARCY WENTWORTH THOMPSON
(1860-1948)
(SCOTTISH ZOOLOGIST, CLASSICAL SCHOLAR)

WALTER

A GENTLE MAN NAMED WALTER
SELLING JEWELRY AT A SHOW
TOUCHED MY HEART PROFOUNDLY
MORE THAN HE COULD POSSIBLY EVER KNOW

A PENDANT WITH A DOLPHIN
CAUGHT MY EYE AS I WALKED BY
IT WAS SPECIAL - SET IN CRYSTAL
I LOOKED UP AND HE SAID HI

CAN I ANSWER ANY QUESTIONS
HE ASKED AS I STOOD AND STARED
I WOULD LOVE TO BUY THIS PENDANT
COULD I TELL HIM, DID I DARE

I'M COMPLETELY OUT OF MONEY
AND I'VE USED UP MY LAST CHECK
HE SAID SEND IT TO ME LATER
AND PUT THE PENDANT 'ROUND MY NECK

THOUGH IT'S HOW HE MAKES HIS LIVING
MONEY'S NOT HIS ULTIMATE GOAL
HE TOUCHED ONE LIFE WITH LOVE AND TRUST
THE TRUE ESSENCE OF HIS SOUL

JUST IN CASE YOU'RE WONDERING
WHETHER WALTER GOT HIS DOUGH
I MAILED IT OUT THE NEXT DAY
NO ONE NEEDS ANOTHER FOE

NO AQUARIUM, NO TANK IN A MARINELAND, HOWEVER
SPACIOUS IT MAY BE, CAN BEGIN TO DUPLICATE THE
CONDITIONS OF THE SEA. AND NO DOLPHIN WHO
INHABITS THEM CAN BE CONSIDERED "NORMAL".
- JACQUES COUSTEAU

THE THREAD OF LIGHT

THE CARRYOVER SOUL REMEMBERS
THAT WHICH WILL HELP THIS TIME AROUND
WHEN SNIPPETS OF MEMORY PEEK THROUGH THE VEIL
A SMALL PART OF OUR PAST HAS BEEN FOUND

EACH SOUL BELONGS TO THE UNIVERSE
A FRAGMENT OF A DISTANT STAR
THROUGH THE MEMORY OF THIS THREAD OF LIGHT
WE AWAKEN TO THE POWER THAT WE ARE

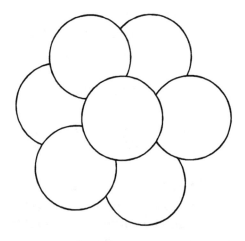

THERE IS ONE THING STRONGER THAN ALL THE ARMIES
OF THE WORLD, AND THAT IS AN IDEA WHOSE TIME
HAS COME.
                                    - VICTOR HUGO

LIFELINE

WE ARE ALL ONE HUMANITY
WE CANNOT LIVE IN GREED
TO SHARE THE EARTH'S POSSESSIONS
MUST NOW BECOME OUR CREED

THERE'S FOOD ENOUGH FOR EVERYONE
AND ENERGY GALORE
ELIMINATE COMPLACENCY
START THINKING LESS NOT MORE

DEPLETION OF RESOURCES
IS EVERY NATION'S FAULT
AWARENESS OF THE HUMAN MIND
WILL BRING IT TO A HALT

OUR WORLD IS COMPRISED OF
EVERYONE'S BACK YARD
LOOK BEYOND YOUR FENCE LINE
SEE THAT MANY LIVES ARE MARRED

DO NOT BECOME SO BUSY
THAT YOU HAVEN'T TIME TO CARE
PLEASE REALIZE EARTH'S LIFE DEPENDS
UPON OUR WILLINGNESS TO SHARE

THE DREAMER

DREAMS ARE MASTERS AT CONQUERING FEAR
DARING THE DREAMER TO SEE AND HEAR
WHY AN AVERSION TO BEING UP HIGH
WHEN THERE ARE REALMS LIKE AN EAGLE I FLY

WATER CONTAINS SUCH TERROR OF THE DEEP
THOUGH I SWIM UNAFRAID WITH DOLPHINS IN SLEEP
BY BLENDING REALITIES WITH BALANCE AND PEACE
TRUST ASSURES THAT FEAR IS RELEASED

IN SLEEP, THE KING IS NO GREATER THAN THE
BEGGAR.
- ALICE O. HOWELL
THE WEB IN THE SEA

JUDAS

I HAD TO LEARN THE HARD WAY
TO DISTINGUISH FRIEND FROM FOE
AT TIMES A BIT TOO TRUSTING
OF EVEN THOSE I DO NOT KNOW

ON A TRIP WITH PEERS OF LIKE MIND
I THOUGHT ALL WERE HONEST AND KIND
BUT, ONE JUDAS WAS AMONG US
I WAS TO VERY SHORTLY FIND

THE DOOR WAS LEFT WIDE OPEN
INVITING VISITORS AT THE INN
WE WERE ALL ONE HAPPY FAMILY
YOU DON'T STEAL FROM YOUR OWN 'KIN'

THERE WAS VALUE IN THIS LESSON
AND THE STAKES WEREN'T VERY HIGH
GUESS JUDAS AND I WERE SUPPOSED TO MEET
TO SEVER THIS KARMIC TIE

●
● ●

WHEN YOU HAVE BEEN COMPELLED BY
CIRCUMSTANCES TO BE DISTURBED IN ANY MANNER,
QUICKLY RETURN TO YOURSELF, AND DO NOT
CONTINUE OUT OF TUNE LONGER THAN THE
COMPULSION LASTS. YOU WILL HAVE INCREASING
CONTROL OVER YOUR OWN HARMONY BY CONTINUALLY
RETURNING TO IT.

MARCUS AURELIUS

CRITICAL MASS

THE MAJORITY OF MANKIND IS LOVING
THOUGH SOME FERTILIZE NEGATIVE SEEDS
WHY NOT CONCENTRATE MORE ON THE POSITIVE
STARTING WITH OUR OWN THOUGHTS AND DEEDS

ONE PERSON CAN MAKE ALL THE DIFFERENCE
HARD WORK CAN CHANGE 'FAIL' TO 'PASS'
OUR PLANET IS CLOSE TO A NEW EVOLUTION
WE ONLY NEED ONE FOR CRITICAL MASS

HOW MANY NEGATIVE THINKERS HAVE YOU BEEN
INSPIRED BY LATELY?
                                    - ANGEL WISDOM

STONED

THE VIBRATION OF STONE IS SOOTHING
PENETRATING THE HEART AND MIND
WHETHER USED FOR MEDITATION OR HEALING
I'M GRATEFUL FOR EVERY KIND

THESE LIVING OBJECTS OF WONDER
WITH THEIR VARIOUS COLORS AND SHAPES
COMMAND OUR ATTENTION WHEN SEARCHING
IN STORES, NEAR MOUNTAINS OR LAKES

HAVE YOU EVER WONDERED WHY YOU CHOSE
FROM ALL THE ZILLIONS OF STONES
TO PICK UP ONE THAT CALLED YOUR NAME
GUESS YOU COULD FEEL IT IN YOUR BONES

 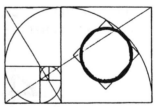

IT IS PERHAPS A MORE FORTUNATE DESTINY TO HAVE
A TASTE FOR COLLECTING SHELLS THAN TO BE BORN
A MILLIONAIRE.
- ROBERT LOUIS STEVENSON
(1850-1894)
(SCOTTISH ESSAYIST, NOVELIST, AND POET)

SIMPLY COMPLEX

A MAN CAMPING WITH FRIENDS ON MT. SHASTA
APPROACHED OUR GROUP ONE DAY
HE ASKED FOR FILM FOR HIS CAMERA
BUT WAS SORRY HE COULDN'T PAY

AFTER PAUSING FOR ONLY A MOMENT
OUR FRIEND JONATHAN DID HIS PART
IN RETURN HE WAS GIVEN A WONDERFUL TAPE
RECIPROCAL ENERGY WAS EXCHANGED FROM THE HEART

SUCH CONTENTMENT AND LOVE SHONE ON THE MAN'S FACE
THOUGH HE DIDN'T HAVE A DIME
YOU COULD SENSE THE COMPLEXITY OF HIS SOUL
MIXED WITH A SIMPLE LIFE THIS TIME

AS HE CONTINUED UP THE MOUNTAIN
DISAPPEARING INTO THE LAND
I RECOGNIZED THE LIGHT OF CHRIST
IN THIS GENTLE, PEACEFUL MAN

WHEREVER THE SAGE IS, HE TEACHES WITHOUT WORDS.

- LAO-TZU,
TAO TEH CHING

EYE WONDER

MET-A-PHYSICAL WHAT

SOMETIMES EYE WONDER

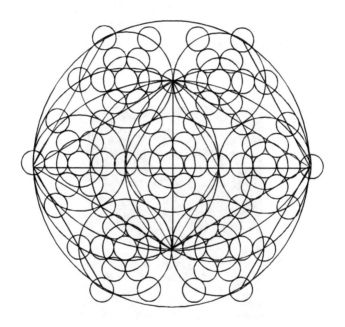

THE FEELING OF AWE AND SENSE OF WONDER ARISES
FROM THE RECOGNITION OF THE DEEP MYSTERY THAT
SURROUNDS US EVERYWHERE. AND THIS FEELING
DEEPENS AS OUR KNOWLEDGE GROWS.

— ANAGARIKE GOVINDA

STAR GAZING

TO SIT ON TOP OF A MOUNTAIN
AND WATCH THE STARS AT NIGHT
WHERE SOME REACH THE TIPS OF YOUR FINGERS
IS A TRULY AMAZING SIGHT

THE SKY IS SPECTACULAR
ITS BLACKNESS SHINY AND VAST
JUST ONE OF MANY OF NATURE'S DELIGHTS
TO ENJOY WITHOUT USING CASH

HE IS INVITED TO GREAT THINGS WHO RECEIVES SMALL
THINGS GREATLY.
- FLAVIUS
(490-583)
(ROMAN LEGAL WRITER AND POLITICIAN)

WORD POWER

WORDS ARE VERY POWERFUL
WE CAN USE THEM TO HARM OR HEAL
IF SOMEONE SPOKE YOUR WORDS TO YOU
HOW WOULD YOU HONESTLY FEEL

MANY WORDS LEAD ONE NOWHERE. MANY PURSUITS IN
DIFFERENT DIRECTIONS BRING ONLY EXHAUSTION.
RATHER, EMBRACE THE SUBTLE ESSENCE WITHIN.
- LAO-TZU

CHAMELEON

RELEASE FEAR
BEGIN TO SEE
A CHANGE WITHIN
FROM ME TO WE

WE HAVE A CHOICE
IN HOW WE LIVE
WITH OPEN HEARTS
CHOOSE LOVE TO GIVE

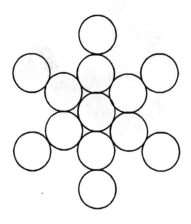

THEY CAN BECAUSE THEY THINK THEY CAN.
- VIRGIL

BENJAMIN

ENERGY PULSATING
HEALING FROM A FRIEND
UNEXPECTED VOLTAGE
HEARTS RACING LIKE THE WIND

MEMORIES OF LONG AGO
BLEND WITH AN AUTUMN DAY
ONE SMALL DAISY WAVING
KEEP THE SPARKS AT BAY

A DEEP SOUL CONNECTION
REFLECTS IN THE EYES
IN THIS PRESENT LIFETIME
THERE ARE OTHER TIES

BEAUTY STIRS THE MOMENT
JOY FLOODS THE HEART
SADNESS FINDS TWO BEINGS
ONCE MORE TORN APART

WERE THERE ANCIENT JOURNEYS
WHAT SECRETS DID WE TEND
WILL I KNOW BY MORNING
WHO IS BENJAMIN

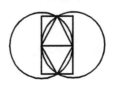

WE'RE ONLY ONE PLANET

THE UNIVERSE DOESN'T BELONG TO MAN
MAN BELONGS TO THE UNIVERSE
WILL MANKIND HONOR THIS SIMPLE TRUTH
OR CONTINUE TO LET THINGS GET WORSE

A WISE MAN KNEW THIS LONG AGO
HE SAW THE DESTRUCTION OF BATTLE
AND THAT CHAOS REIGNS WITHOUT RESPECT
THIS VISIONARY WAS CHIEF SEATTLE

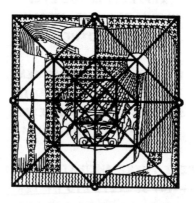

FORCE WITHOUT WISDOM FALLS OF ITS OWN WEIGHT.

- HORACE
65 B.C.-8 B.C.
(ROMAN POET AND SATIRIST)

DIGGING UP THE PAST

WHEN ANTHROPOLOGISTS LOOK BACK
A MILLION YEARS FROM NOW
IF WE DON'T GET OUR ACT TOGETHER
THEIR REACTION WILL BE 'HOLY COW'

THE GREAT FRENCH MARSHALL LYAUTEY ONCE ASKED
HIS GARDENER TO PLANT A TREE. THE GARDENER
OBJECTED THAT THE TREE WAS SLOW GROWING AND
WOULD NOT REACH MATURITY FOR 100 YEARS. THE
MARSHALL REPLIED, "IN THAT CASE, THERE IS NO TIME
TO LOSE; PLANT IT THIS AFTERNOON."
- J. F. KENNEDY

HEALTHY BOUNDARIES

THE MEDICAL COMMUNITY'S A POWERFUL FORCE
WITH THE TASK OF HEALING THE ILL
THEY KNOW ABOUT LIFE, BUT LITTLE OF HEALTH
FOR EACH ACHE AND PAIN THERE'S A PILL

DO YOU KNOW HOW FEW NUTRITIONAL CLASSES
ARE REQUIRED TO BECOME AN M.D.
TRUE HEALTH CARE WILL CHANGE THE FOCUS
TO WELLNESS INSTEAD OF DIS-EASE

THERE ARE SOME VERY INTERESTING METHODS
SUCH AS LIGHT, COLOR, AND SOUND
THAT ARE NOW BEING USED FOR HEALING
AND WORKING WONDERS IT'S BEEN FOUND

WILL MAINSTREAM MEDICINE ACKNOWLEDGE
TREATING PEOPLE WITH THEIR MISSING NOTES
OR WILL EGO CONTINUE TO DENY ANCIENT TRUTHS
AS MANY OF US FLOAT THESE "NEW" BOATS

IN HEALTH CARE WE HAVE THE RIGHT
TO CHOOSE THE CATEGORY OF "OTHER"
SO LEARN AND WORK WITH THE NEW PIONEERS
WE DON'T NEED ANOTHER BIG BROTHER

---

*MEDICINE IS NOT ONLY A SCIENCE, BUT ALSO THE ART
OF LETTING OUR OWN INDIVIDUALITY INTERACT WITH
THE INDIVIDUALITY OF THE PATIENT.*
- ALBERT SCHWEITZER

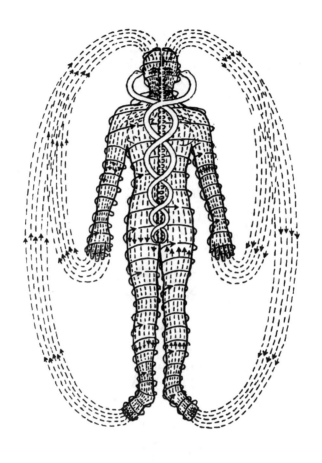

THE DOCTOR OF THE FUTURE WILL GIVE NO MEDICINE,
BUT WILL INTEREST HIS PATIENT IN THE CARE OF THE
HUMAN FRAME, IN DIET, AND IN THE PREVENTION OF
DISEASE.

- THOMAS A. EDISON

BIJA MANTRA

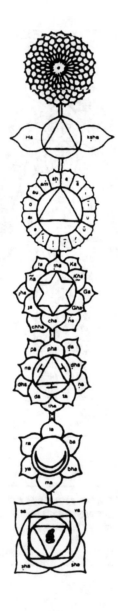

THE BIJA-MANTRAS ARE THE MOST POTENT OF ALL. THEY DEFINITELY BELONG TO NO LANGUAGE AND ARE NOT FOUND IN ANY DICTIONARY. THEY HAVE NO GENDER AND DECLENSIONS. THEY ARE COMBINATIONS OF LETTERS THAT REPRESENT THE RELATIONSHIP BETWEEN THE KUNDALINI (LIFE ENERGY) AND THE SUPREME CONSCIOUSNESS (SACRED SOUND), AND THEIR SPECIFIC RAYS (ELEMENTAL ARCHETYPES)...AN ATTEMPT TO UNDERSTAND THEM INTELLECTUALLY WILL BE FUTILE.

-USHARBUDH ARYA
MUSIC & SOUND IN HEALING ARTS
BY JOHN BEAULIEU

GOING, GOING, GONE

THE MIND
IS THE GREATEST
TRAVEL AGENT

OH! I HAVE SLIPPED THE SURLY BONDS OF EARTH AND
DANCED THE SKIES ON LAUGHTER-SILVERED WINGS...

- JOHN G. MAGEE, JR.

THE DREAM WEAVER

THE DREAM WEAVER CALLS THE ROLL
AS EYES FLY OPEN WIDE
BEGIN THE MIDNIGHT VOYAGE
RIDING POSSIBILITY ASTRIDE

THE TREASURE CHEST SITS GLEAMING
A SOUL UNFOLDS ITS WINGS
AND TRAVELS THROUGH THE UNIVERSE
ON A HEART WITH SILVER STRINGS

ENVELOPED IN A SEA OF BLISS
A RADIANT BEING CRIES
ABSORBED BY SYNCHRONICITY
IN THE TWINKLING OF AN EYE

REGAINING MY SIGHT

HOW CAN I BLINDLY TRUST
WHAT EVEN SCHOLARS DON'T UNDERSTAND
THE DOCTRINE OF RELIGION
PASSED DOWN FROM MAN TO MAN

FREEDOM FORMS A PAIR OF WINGS
AS I UNDO OLD TIES
IN MY CONSTANT SEARCH FOR TRUTH
I FLY THE FRIENDLY SKIES

WE DON'T GET ANY EDUCATION IN THE UNIVERSITY OR
CHURCH OR EVEN MODERN HOMES TODAY WHICH
LEAD US INWARD.   SO A PART OF LIFE REMAINS
UNREVEALED TO US, AND WE ONLY GET THE HUSK OF
LIFE.

— SWAMMI RAMA

SOPHIA

SOPHIA IS A HOLY SPIRIT. SOPHIA IS COMFORTER,
KIND, ACTIVE, WELL-MEANING, WELL-DOING, ALL-
POWERFUL. SOPHIA IS A TRANSFORMER, ONE SO PURE
THAT SHE PERVADES AND PERMEATES ALL THINGS.
SOPHIA IS FOUND BY THOSE WHO SEEK HER. JUST
THINKING ABOUT HER BRINGS UNDERSTANDING. SHE
WILL APPEAR TO YOU WHEN YOU SEEK HER, COMING
TO MEET YOU IN YOUR EVERY THOUGHT.
                              - PARAPHRASED FROM
                                THE WISDOM OF SOLOMON

REUNITED

A THOUSAND YEARS
WAITING
NOW KNOWING
THE PURPOSE

TO MEET
FRAGMENTS OF MYSELF
SCATTERED
ALL OVER THE GLOBE

VIBRATIONS
OF LOVE
WRAPPED
IN ETERNITY
REUNITE
AS
PAST LIVES
CIRCLE THE WHEEL
REMEMBERING

TENDERNESS RESPONDS
MAGNETIZED
UNTIL
ONCE MORE
TORN APART

HOW
CAN A SHATTERED HEART
STILL FEEL
SUCH PAIN

UNTIL WE MEET AGAIN
MY FRIEND
BE HAPPY

REMEMBER
IN LAK'ECH

NEXT TIME
LET'S NOT WAIT
A THOUSAND YEARS

IN THE TIME OF GATHERING TOGETHER, MAKE NO
ARBITRARY CHOICE OF YOUR ASSOCIATES. THERE ARE
SECRET FORCES AT WORK, LEADING TOGETHER THOSE
WHO BELONG TOGETHER.
— I CHING WISDOM

MONKEY BUSINESS

A RESOUNDING ROAR FROM THE JUNGLE
GREETS THE SILENCE OF PALENQUE
THE DREAMTIME WELCOMES A CHORUS
OF PASSIONATE JAGUAR MONKEYS

THEIR FAMILIAR BELLOW IS SOOTHING
MEMORIES STIR TO AWAKEN ONCE MORE
A SLEEPY SMILE CONNECTS THE HEART
TO A SOUL THAT'S BEEN HERE BEFORE

THE GEOMETRIC DRAWINGS GIVE THE IMPRESSION OF
A CIPHER-SCRIPT IN WHICH THE SAME WORDS ARE
SOMETIMES WRITTEN IN HUGE LETTERS, AT ANOTHER
TIME IN MINUTE CHARACTERS. THERE ARE LINE
ARRANGEMENTS WHICH APPEAR IN A GREAT VARIETY
OF SIZE CATEGORIES TOGETHER WITH VERY SIMILAR
SHAPES. ALL THE DRAWINGS ARE COMPOSED OF A
CERTAIN NUMBER OF BASIC ELEMENTS...
- MARIA REICHE
MATHEMATICIAN

THE DISGUISE

DISGUISED AS THE UNKNOWN
LOVE'S SHADOW APPEARS
AS THE MYSTERY OF VIBRATION
UNWINDS THE CLOCK
OF ILLUSION

UNSEEN ENERGY
DOES ITS JOB
TESTING

ENDLESSLY CREATIVE,
LOVE
REINVENTS ITSELF,
MAKING US CHOOSE
BETWEEN IT
AND FEAR

IN THE END
THE SOUL SMILES
KNOWING
IT WAS A TEST,
IT WAS ONLY A TEST

I BELIEVE THAT IN THE END TRUTH WILL CONQUER.
- JOHN WYCLIFFE, 1334

THE IMAGE OF LOVE

MAN WAS CREATED IN GOD'S IMAGE
WE'VE ALL HEARD THIS BEFORE
IN FACT, WHILE TRYING TO PROVE THIS
MANY HAVE GONE TO WAR

WHAT ABOUT UNIVERSAL MAN
HIS CREATOR IS ALSO THE DOVE
MAYBE GOD'S IMAGE HAS NO FACE
WHAT WE 'SEE' IS THE SPIRIT OF LOVE

...IT'S STRANGE HOW MANY PEOPLE ONLY PICTURE GOD AS TRANSCENDENT, MAKING HIMSELF KNOWN BY SHOOTING OFF THUNDERBOLTS. GOD IS TRANSCENDENT, ABOVE THE WORLD AND BEYOND IT, OUTSIDE TIME AND SPACE IN A MODE OF BEING WHICH IS BEYOND THE SCOPE OF OUR IMAGINATIONS TO CONCEIVE, BUT THE GOD WHO MAKES HIMSELF KNOWN TO US IS THE IMMANENT GOD, THE GOD WHO'S SO CLOSE THAT HE'S AT THE VERY CENTER OF OUR EXISTENCE. IT'S STRANGE TOO HOW MUCH TIME PEOPLE SPEND TRAVELLING ROUND AND ROUND THE CIRCLE OF EXISTENCE AND GETTING NOWHERE. THE REAL JOURNEY - THE JOURNEY ALL PEOPLE ARE REQUIRED TO TAKE TO ACHIEVE INTEGRATION, SELF-REALISATION, AND FULFILLMENT - "THE ETERNAL LIFE" OF RELIGIOUS LANGUAGE-IS THE JOURNEY INWARDS, THE JOURNEY TO THE CENTRE OF THE SOUL.

-SUSAN HOWATCH, 1992

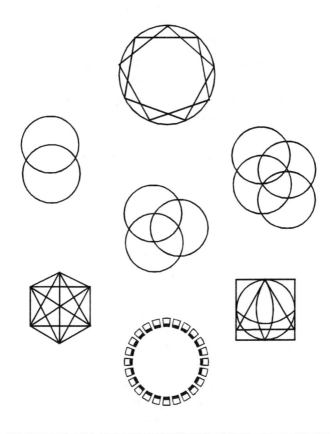

THE GEOMETER'S AIM, THEREFORE IS TO IMITATE THE
UNIVERSE SYMBOLICALLY, DEPICTING ITS CENTRAL
PARADOX BY BRINGING TOGETHER SHAPES OF
DIFFERENT GEOMETRIC ORDERS; UNITING THEM AS
SIMPLY AND ACCURATELY AS POSSIBLE AND THUS
CREATING A COSMIC IMAGE.

— JOHN MICHELL

ALL OUR RELATIONS

OVERFLOWING,
A HEART SPILLS ITS TEARS
FOR THE NEXT SEVEN GENERATIONS
FOR LIFEFORMS NOW EXTINCT,
FOR SILENT SONGS,
FOR BEAUTY WHOSE EYES ARE CLOSED
NEVER TO SEE OR BE SEEN AGAIN

WILL OUR LIGHT GROW BRIGHT
OR DIM
WILL OUR CHILDREN
RUN TOWARD THE FUTURE
WITH OUTSTRETCHED ARMS
OF HOPE
OR HOBBLE
UNDER THE BURDEN OF DISPAIR

EVERY THOUGHT,
EVERY CHOICE,
EVERY WORD,
EVERY ACTION,
EVERY REACTION
MATTERS

ETERNITY
IS SUPPOSED TO BE
FOREVER
FOR ALL OUR RELATIONS

NOW THIS, MONKS, IS THE NOBLE TRUTH OF THE WAY
THAT LEADS TO THE CESSATION OF SORROW: THIS IS
THE NOBLE EIGHTFOLD WAY: NAMELY, RIGHT VIEWS,
RIGHT INTENTION, RIGHT SPEECH, RIGHT ACTION,
RIGHT LIVELIHOOD, RIGHT EFFORT, RIGHT
MINDFULNESS, RIGHT CONCENTRATION.

- BUDDHA

DIVINE INFLUENCE

AS ANOTHER GREAT CYCLE OF TIME DRAWS TO A CLOSE, THE DAWN OF A NEW UNDERSTANDING ILLUMINATES THE HORIZON: HUMANITY WILL ASSUME ITS PROPER PLACE IN THE SCHEME OF THINGS AS CO-CREATORS OF THE WORLD ABOUT US. A VOLUNTARY RETURN TO DIVINE LAW. THE MEMORIES THAT ARE NOW STIRRING WITHIN EVERY INDIVIDUAL ARE A RESPONSE TO NEW ENERGIES FLOODING INTO THE EARTH'S FIELD: IT IS FOR EACH PERSON TO BECOME CONSCIOUS OF THEIR ROLE IN THIS GREAT WORK AND PARTICIPATE IN THE PROCESS OF EVOLUTION.

- HAMISH MILLER & PAUL BROADHURST
FROM THE SUN AND THE SERPENT

A HAIR RAISING EXPERIENCE

LONG HAIR,
TIED TO TRADITION,
BRAIDED IN SACRED TRUTH,
STILL MISUNDERSTOOD
BY WHITE MAN
JUDGING HIS HERITAGE

POVERTY CLAIMS HIS LIFE
BUT NOT HIS SPIRIT
AS THE PATH OF ILLUSION
LAYS THE FOUNDATION
TO ONE DAY PAVE
HIS RED ROAD CHOICE

1897
CLAIMED VICTORY
OF SHEARED STRENGTH
WHERE SILENCED LANGUAGE
SPOKE THROUGH EYES
DIMMED BY GRIEF
WHERE BONDAGE TO WHISKEY,
DISEASE,
AND ENTRAPMENT
IN UNFAMILIAR PLACES
CALLED BOARDING SCHOOLS,
PRISONS,
AND RESERVATIONS
HASTENED THE JOURNEY
ON THE BLUE ROAD
HOME

221

1997
ATTEMPTS TO IMPRISON THE SOUL
BY THE LOSS OF JOBS
AND SENSELESS COURT BATTLES
FOR REFUSING TO IGNORE
THE HONOR AND INTEGRITY
OF THE ANCESTORS,
THE ANCIENT ONES

BEHIND THE ATTIRE
OF SHORT HAIRED,
CONSERVATIVE,
CORPORATE AMERICA
HIDES EGO,
ARROGANCE, RUTHLESSNESS,
JUDGMENT,
NON-ACCEPTANCE,
AND ABUSE OF POWER
WHERE THE ODOR OF CONTEMPT
FOR THOSE WHO ARE "DIFFERENT"
SUFFOCATES INTEGRITY
AND COMPASSION

CENTURIES OF TIME
HAS STOOD STILL
TO THE PROGRESS
OF UNDERSTANDING
AND ACCEPTANCE
AS NATIVE AMERICANS
CONTINUE TO FEEL
THE STING OF PREJUDICE

IN AT LEAST ONE
OF THESE UNITED STATES,
OHIO,
IT IS STILL ILLEGAL
TO BE NATIVE AMERICAN

WHO WILL LISTEN,
WHO WILL CARE
ABOUT THIS NATIVE SOUL
WHO CRADLES THE HEART
OF OUR BEAUTIFUL EARTH MOTHER
IN EVERY FIBER OF HIS BEING

WHAT DOES IT MATTER
THE LENGTH OF ONE'S HAIR
IN THIS LAND OF THE FREE,
WHERE FREEDOM OF SPEECH,
FREEDOM OF THE PRESS,
FREEDOM OF EXPRESSION
AND FREEDOM OF RELIGION
REIGNS SUPREME...
OR DOES IT

WHERE IS
THE JUSTICE FOR ALL
OR IS ALL AN ILLUSION

---

*NEVER DOUBT THAT A SMALL GROUP OF THOUGHTFUL,
COMMITTED CITIZENS CAN CHANGE THE WORLD.
INDEED, IT'S THE ONLY THING THAT EVER HAS.*
- MARGARET MEAD

IN DEW TIME

RAINDROPS OF NECTAR
ZOOM IN ON THE BULLSEYE
SPRAYING THE LANDSCAPE
WITH MANNA FROM HEAVEN

INHALE THE AROMA
AWAKENING THE SPRINGTIME
CLEANSING THE EARTH
ONCE MORE NOURISHING LIFE

TRICKLING SOUNDS
INVITE HAPPY CHILDREN
SPLASHING THE LAUGHTER
TONGUES CAPTURING PEARLS

REFRESHING BREEZES
CARESS THE YOUNG PLAYERS
ABSORBING THE MOMENT
TRANSFORMED BY THE MIST

RECEDING SHOWERS
EVENTUALLY GIVE WAY
TO ANOTHER CARETAKER
RENEWER OF LIFE

IN DEW TIME SUNBEAMS
BREATHE RAYS OF ASSURANCE
RESUMING PLAY
OF A BALLGAME DELAYED

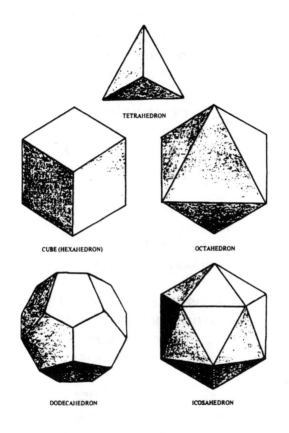

TETRAHEDRON

CUBE (HEXAHEDRON)

OCTAHEDRON

DODECAHEDRON

ICOSAHEDRON

IF WE ARE TO REACH REAL PEACE IN THE WORLD, WE SHALL HAVE TO BEGIN WITH CHILDREN.

— GANDHI

MAGICAL MOMENTS

THE TOUCH OF A BUTTERFLY
RESTING ON LAMBS EAR
ENJOYING THE GRACEFUL
STILLNESS OF MORNING

THE TICKLE OF SPIRIT
WHISPERING ITS WISDOM
TO DOWNY SOFT FEATHERS
SEEKING RANDOM NEW PLACES

SENSATIONAL HEART STONES
GLISTENING LIKE RAINBOWS
HUMMING IN SILENCE
VIBRATIONS OF LOVE

THE SIGHT OF A DRAGONFLY
DARTING THROUGH GRASSES
CATCHING IN MID AIR
A BREAKFAST OF SUNLIGHT

THE VISION OF DAISIES
BRUSHING THE LANDSCAPE
PETALS DANCING IN UNION
ON CARPETED BREEZES

THE RUSH OF A MILL STREAM
SWIRLING AND SPLASHING
JOINING THE MIST
TO PLAY HIDE AND SEEK

CHOIRS OF FROGS AND CRICKETS
AWAKENING THE NIGHTTIME
SINGING THEIR LOVE SONGS
WHILE BATHING IN MOONLIGHT

DISTANT CALLS OF A HOOT OWL
KEEPING WATCH ON THE DREAMTIME
PREPARING THE SHADOWS
TO DAWN A NEW DAY

SACRED SPACE IS WITHIN US. NOT IN OUR BODY OR
BRAIN CELLS BUT IN THE VOLUME OF OUR
CONSCIOUSNESS. WHEREVER WE GO WE BRING THE
SACRED WITHIN US TO THE SACRED AROUND US.

- MICHAEL S. SCHNEIDER
A BEGINNER'S GUIDE TO
CONSTRUCTING THE UNIVERSE

THE BIRTH OF MYSTERY

THE EGG OF MYSTERY
BIRTHS THE DREAMS
OF FUTURE GENERATIONS
WHOSE EYES REFLECT HOPE
ONCE THOUGHT EXTINCT

WRAPPED IN ETERNITY,
KNOWLEDGE IS RESCUED
BY WISDOM
FROM AN OCEAN OF TEARS
TO ONCE AGAIN
EXPLORE THE MOMENT

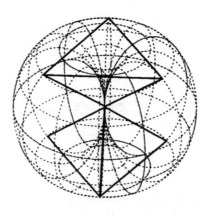

THAT DAY, WHICH YOU FEAR AS BEING THE END OF ALL
THINGS, IS THE BIRTHDAY OF YOUR ETERNITY.
- SENECA

THE MAYAN CALENDAR

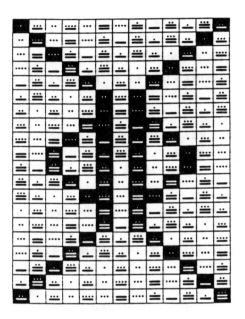

THE 20 SIGNS ARE MODIFIED BY THE 13 POWERS,
CREATING A MATRIX OF 260 COMBINATIONS. DARK
SQUARES ARE THE 52-UNIT HARMONIC MATRIX THAT IS
FORMED BY SETS OF SQUARES THAT HAVE A
COMBINED VALUE OF 28, THE AVERAGE NUMBER OF
DAYS IN A LUNAR CYCLE.
                              - RICHARD DANNELLEY
                         SEDONA: BEYOND THE VORTEX

THERE ARE NO UNNATURAL OR SUPERNATURAL
PHENOMENA. ONLY VERY LARGE GAPS IN OUR
KNOWLEDGE OF WHAT IS NATURAL...WE SHOULD
STRIVE TO FILL THESE GAPS OF IGNORANCE.
                                  - EDGAR MITCHELL
                             APOLLO 14 ASTRONAUT

MASTERS OF THE LIGHT

SCATTERED CLOUDS RACE DISTANT STARS
ONE IMITATES THE SUN
THE MIDNIGHT SKY ACKNOWLEDGES
MASTERS OF THE LIGHT HAVE COME

MUSIC HUGS THE WOODLAND HILLS
TREES HUM THE SOUND OF OM
FUNNELED RAYS SPROUT FROM THE MOON
ILLUMINATING ANCIENT ONES

UNICORNS AND NATURE SPIRITS
DANCE IN FIELDS OF SPLENDOR
CAPTURING IN OTHER REALMS
THE STILLNESS OF ADVENTURE

METATRON AND MARY
KUAN YIN, HATHOR, RA
LINK FIBERS ONCE CONCEALED
TO THE GATES OF SANGRI-LA

FEARLESS STRENGTH AND GENTLENESS
WEAVE SILK THREADS OF MAGIC
TO SHARE THE WEB IN WEDDED BLISS
WITH MASTERS OF THE LIGHT FANTASTIC

THERE IS NO SAFER PLACE FOR ULTIMATE WISDOM TO
HIDE THAN IN THE OBVIOUS.
- ALICE O. HOWELL
THE WEB IN THE SEA

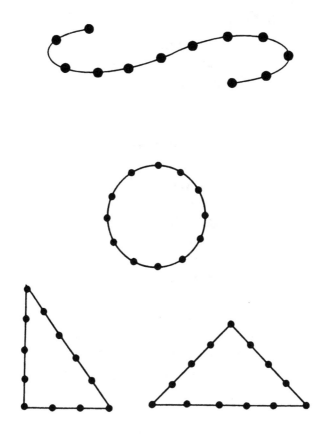

THE "DRUIDS' CORD" WAS USED BY THE EGYPTIANS FOR DESIGNING CONSTRUCTION, SINCE IT CAN FORM A PYTHAGOREAN RIGHT TRIANGLE, A 4, 4, 5 TRIANGLE AND A 12-SPOKE WHEEL.

LABOR OF LOVE

TO WRITE 150 POEMS
WAS THE ORIGINAL GOAL
PREGNANT WITH POSSIBILITIES
THE BALL BEGAN TO ROLL

LIFE HAS BEEN AN ADVENTURE
OF MEMORIES SUSPENDED IN TIME
RHYTHM ENTICED FEELINGS TO SPEAK
RANDOM HUMOR, CANDOR AND RHYME

PASSION CREATED A MULTIPLE BIRTH
RELATING A TRIPLE STORY
BRINGING FORTH A LABOR OF LOVE
IN ALL ITS CROWNING GLORY

SPECIAL ATTENTION TO DETAIL
DISCHARGED EXCESSIVE GIRTH
PUSHING TOWARD THEIR DUE DATE
THE BABIES ARE READY TO BE BIRTHED

THE UNION OF THE MATHEMATICIAN WITH THE POET,
FERVOR WITH MEASURE, PASSION WITH CORRECTNESS,
THIS SURELY IS THE IDEAL.

- WILLIAM JAMES
(1842-1910)
AMERICAN PSYCHOLOGIST AND PHILOSOPHER

FINALLY

THE BOOK IS FINISHED
MY SOUL'S BEEN FED
THE DEADLINE'S MET
ENOUGH SAID

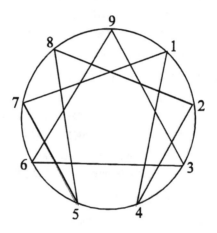

DESIDERATA

❀❀❀ GO PLACIDLY AMID THE NOISE & HASTE, & REMEMBER WHAT PEACE THERE MAY BE IN SILENCE. AS FAR AS POSSIBLE WITHOUT SURRENDER BE ON GOOD TERMS WITH ALL PERSONS. SPEAK YOUR TRUTH QUIETLY & CLEARLY; AND LISTEN TO OTHERS, EVEN THE DULL & IGNORANT; THEY TOO HAVE THEIR STORY. ❀ AVOID LOUD & AGGRESSIVE PERSONS, THEY ARE VEXATIONS TO THE SPIRIT. IF YOU COMPARE YOURSELF WITH OTHERS, YOU MAY BECOME VAIN & BITTER; FOR ALWAYS THERE WILL BE GREATER & LESSER PERSONS THAN YOURSELF.

ENJOY YOUR ACHIEVEMENTS AS WELL AS YOUR PLANS. ❀ KEEP INTERESTED IN YOUR OWN CAREER, HOWEVER HUMBLE; IT IS A REAL POSSESSION IN THE CHANGING FORTUNES OF TIME. EXERCISE CAUTION IN YOUR BUSINESS AFFAIRS; FOR THE WORLD IS FULL OF TRICKERY. BUT LET THIS NOT BLIND YOU TO WHAT VIRTUE THERE IS; MANY PERSONS STRIVE FOR HIGH IDEALS; AND EVERYWHERE LIFE IS FULL OF HEROISM. ❀ BE YOURSELF. ESPECIALLY, DO NOT FEIGN AFFECTION. NEITHER BE CYNICAL ABOUT LOVE; FOR IN THE FACE OF ALL ARIDITY & DISENCHANTMENT IT IS PERENNIAL AS THE GRASS.

❀❀❀ TAKE KINDLY THE COUNSEL OF THE YEARS, GRACEFULLY SURRENDERING THE THINGS OF YOUTH. NURTURE STRENGTH OF SPIRIT TO SHIELD YOU IN SUDDEN MISFORTUNE. BUT DO NOT DISTRESS YOURSELF WITH IMAGININGS. MANY FEARS ARE BORN OF FATIGUE & LONELINESS. BEYOND A WHOLESOME DISCIPLINE, BE GENTLE WITH YOURSELF. YOU ARE A CHILD OF THE UNIVERSE, NO LESS THAN THE TREES & THE STARS; YOU HAVE A RIGHT TO BE HERE. AND WHETHER OR NOT IT IS CLEAR TO YOU, NO DOUBT THE UNIVERSE IS UNFOLDING AS IT

SHOULD. ❋THEREFORE BE AT PEACE WITH GOD, WHATEVER YOU CONCEIVE HIM TO BE, AND WHATEVER YOUR LABORS & ASPIRATIONS, IN THE NOISY CONFUSION OF LIFE KEEP PEACE WITH YOUR SOUL. ❋ WITH ALL ITS SHAM, DRUDGERY & BROKEN DREAMS, IT IS STILL A BEAUTIFUL WORLD. BE CAREFUL. STRIVE TO BE HAPPY.

FOUND IN OLD SAINT PAUL'S CHURCH
BALTIMORE; DATED 1692

ORA ET LABORA, LEGE, LEGE, LEGE ET RELEGE,
ET INVENIES.
(PRAY AND WORK. READ, READ, READ AND
REREAD, AND DISCOVER)

BIBLIOGRAPHY

ANDERSON, GREG. THE CANCER CONQUEROR: AN INCREDIBLE JOURNEY TO WELLNESS. (KANSAS CITY, MO: ANDREWS AND MCMEEL, 1988). ISBN 0-8362-2415-9

ANDREWS, TED. ANIMAL SPEAK: THE SPIRITUAL AND MAGICAL POWERS OF CREATURES GREAT AND SMALL. (ST. PAUL, MN: LLEWELLYN PUBLICATIONS, 1993). ISBN 0-87542-028-1
*

BEAULIEU, JOHN. MUSIC AND SOUND IN THE HEALING ARTS. (BARRYTOWN, NY: STATION HILL PRESS, INC., 1987). ISBN 0-88268-056-0

BERLITZ, CHARLES. ATLANTIS: THE EIGHTH CONTINENT. (N.Y., N.Y.: G. P. PUTNAM'S SONS, 1984). ISBN 0-399-12892-1

BLUM, RALPH. THE BOOK OF RUNES. (N.Y., N.Y.: ST. MARTIN'S PRESS, 1937). ISBN 0-312-00729-9

BRADEN, GREG. AWAKENING TO ZERO POINT: THE COLLECTIVE INITIATION. (BELLEVUE, WA: LL PRODUCTIONS, 1993/1994). ISBN 0-9648990-4-3
*

CANNON, DELORES. LEGACY FROM THE STARS. (HUNTSVILLE, AR: OZARK MOUNTAIN PUBLISHERS, 1996). ISBN 0-9632776-9-3

CHILDRESS, DAVID HATCHER. LOST CITIES OF ATLANTIS, ANCIENT EUROPE & THE MEDITERRANEAN. (STELLE, IL: ADVENTURES UNLIMITED PRESS, 1996). ISBN 0-932813-25-9

CONWAY, D. J. THE ANCIENT AND SHINING ONES. (ST. PAUL, MN: LLEWELLYN PUBLICATIONS, 1993). ISBN 0-87542-170-9
*

DANNELLEY, RICHARD. SEDONA: BEYOND THE VORTEX. (SEDONA, AZ: THE VORTEX SOCIETY, 1995). ISBN 0-9629453-7-4

EGYPTIAN MYSTERIES (YORK BEACH, ME: SAMUEL WEISER, 1988) MATERIAL USED BY PERMISSION. ISBN 0-87728-681-7

FANTHORPE, LIONEL & PATRICIA. SECRETS OF RENNES LE

CHATEAU. (YORK BEACH, ME: SAMUEL WEISER, INC., 1992). ISBN 0-87728-744-9

FRISSELL, BOB. NOTHING IN THIS BOOK IS TRUE, BUT IT'S EXACTLY THE WAY THINGS ARE. (BERKELEY, CA: FROG, LTD, 1994). ISBN 1-883319-01-3

GIBRAN, KAHLIL. THE PROPHET. (N.Y., NY: ALFRED A. KNOPF, INC., 1923). ISBN 0-394-40428-9

GONZALEZ-WIPPLER, MIGENE. THE COMPLETE BOOK OF AMULETS & TALISMANS. (ST. PAUL, MN: LLEWELLYN PUBLICATIONS, 1991). ISBN 0-87542-287-X

GUIRDHAM, ARTHUR. WE ARE ONE ANOTHER: ASTOUNDING EVIDENCE OF GROUP REINCARNATION. (ESSEX, ENGLAND: THE C. W. DANIEL COMPANY LTD, 1974). ISBN 0-85207-248-1
*
HANCOCK, GRAHAM. FINGERPRINTS OF THE GODS: THE EVIDENCE OF EARTH'S LOST CIVILIZATION. ISBN 0-517-88729-0

HANH, THICH NHAT. LIVING BUDDHA, LIVING CHRIST. (N.Y., NY: RIVERHEAD BOOKS, 1995). ISBN 1-57322-018-3

HANH, THICH NHAT. PEACE IS EVERY STEP: THE PATH OF MINDFULNESS IN EVERYDAY LIFE. (N.Y., NY: BANTAM BOOKS, 1991). ISBN 0-553-35139-7

HAYWARD, SUSAN. A GUIDE FOR THE ADVANCED SOUL. (AVALON NSW 2107, AUSTRALIA: IN-TUNE BOOKS, 1984). ISBN 0-9590439-0-X

HAYWARD, SUSAN. BEGIN IT NOW. (AVALON NSW 2107, AUSTRALIA: IN-TUNE BOOKS, 1987). ISBN 0-9590439-1-8

HOAGLAND, RICHARD C. THE MONUMENTS OF MARS: A CITY ON THE EDGE OF FOREVER, 4TH ED. (BERKELEY, CA: FROG, LTD., 1996). ISBN 1-883319-30-7

HOWELL, ALICE O. THE WEB IN THE SEA: JUNG, SOPHIA, AND THE GEOMETRY OF THE SOUL. (WHEATON, IL: QUEST

BOOKS, 1993). ISBN 0-8356-0688-0

HOWELL, ALICE O. *THE DOVE IN THE STONE: FINDING THE SACRED IN THE COMMONPLACE.* (WHEATON, IL: QUEST BOOKS, 1988). ISBN 0-8356-0639-2

JOHNSTON, CHARLES. *YOGA SUTRAS OF PATANJALI.* (ALBUQUERQUE, NM: BROTHERHOOD OF LIFE, INC., 1912). ISBN 0-914732-08-0

JOSEPH, FRANK. *ATLANTIS IN WISCONSIN: NEW REVELATIONS ABOUT LOST SUNKEN CITY.* (ST. PAUL, MN: GALDE PRESS, INC., 1995). ISBN 1-880090-12-0

*

MASON, JEFFREY MOUSSAIEFF, AND MCCARTHY, SUSAN. *WHEN ELEPHANTS WEEP: THE EMOTIONAL LIVES OF ANIMALS.* (N. Y., NY: DELACORTE PRESS, 1995). ISBN 0-385-31425-6

MILLER, HAMISH AND PAUL BROADHURST. *THE SUN AND THE SERPENT: AN INVESTIGATION INTO EARTH ENERGIES.* (CORNWALL, UNITED KINGDOM: PENDRAGON PRESS, 1994 NEW EDITION). ISBN 0-9515183-1-3

MING-DAO, DENG. *365 TAO: DAILY MEDITATIONS.* (N.Y., NY: HARPERCOLLINS, 1992. ISBN 0-06-250223-9

NI, HUA-CHING. *THE COMPLETE WORKS OF LAO TZU: TAO TEH CHING & HUA HU CHING.* (SANTA MONICA, CA: SEVEN STAR COMMUNICATIONS GROUP, 1979). ISBN 0-937064-00-9

OLSEN, CYNTHIA AND DR. JIM CHAN. *ESSIAC, A HERBAL CANCER REMEDY.* (PAGOSA SPRINGS, CO: KALI PRESS, 1996). ISBN 0-9628882-5-7

RAINBOW EAGLE. *THE UNIVERSAL PEACE SHIELD OF TRUTHS: ANCIENT AMERICAN INDIAN PEACE SHIELD TEACHINGS.* (ANGEL FIRE, NM: RAINBOW LIGHT AND COMPANY, 1996). ISBN 0-9655217-0-2

RINPOCHE, SOGYAL. *THE TIBETAN BOOK OF LIVING AND DYING.* (N.Y., NY: HARPERCOLLINS, 1993). ISBN 0-06-250834-2

SAMS, JAMIE. SACRED PATH CARDS: THE DISCOVERY OF SELF THROUGH NATIVE TEACHINGS. (N. Y., NY: HARPERCOLLINS, 1990). ISBN 0-06-250762-1

*

SCHNEIDER, MICHAEL S. A BEGINNERS GUIDE TO CONSTRUCTING THE UNIVERSE: THE MATHEMATICAL ARCHETYPES OF NATURE, ART, AND SCIENCE. (N. Y., NY: HARPERCOLLINS, 1994). ISBN 0-06-092671-6

SMITH, P. DAVID. OURAY, CHIEF OF THE UTES. (RIDGEWAY, CO: WAYFINDER PRESS, 1986). ISBN 0-9608764-4-8

TAYLOR, TERRY LYNN AND MARY BETH CRAIN. ANGEL WISDOM: 365 MEDITATIONS AND INSIGHTS FROM THE HEAVENS. (N. Y., NY: HARPERCOLLINS, 1994). ISBN 0-06-251067-3

WALKER, BARBARA G. WOMAN'S DICTIONARY OF SYMBOLS AND SACRED OBJECTS. (N. Y., NY: HARPERCOLLINS, 1988). ISBN 0-06-250923-3

WALSCH, NEALE DONALD. CONVERSATIONS WITH GOD - BOOK I - AN UNCOMMON DIALOG. (CHARLOTTESVILLE, VA: HAMPTON ROADS, 1995). ISBN 1-57174-025-2

WATSON, DONALD. THE DICTIONARY OF MIND AND SPIRIT. (N.Y., NY: AVON BOOKS, 1991). ISBN 0-380-71792-1

WESSELMAN, HANK. SPIRITWALKER: MESSAGES FROM THE FUTURE. (N. Y., NY: BANTAM BOOKS, 1995). ISBN 0-553-09976-0

WIGMORE, ANN. THE WHEATGRASS BOOK. (WAYNE, NJ: AVERY PUBLISHING GROUP, INC., 1985). ISBN 0-89529-234-3

WEI, WU. I CHING WISDOM: GUIDANCE FROM THE BOOK OF WISDOM. (LOS ANGELES, CA: POWER PRESS, 1994). ISBN 0-943015-03-0

WILLIAMS, MARY, ED. GLASTONBURY & BRITAIN: A STUDY IN PATTERNS. (ORPINGTON, KENT, ENGLAND: R.I.L.K.O. BOOKS, 1990). ISBN 0-902103-14-8.

* ADDITIONAL BIBLIOGRAPHY

ANDREWS, TED. SACRED SOUNDS: TRANSFORMATION THROUGH MUSIC & WORD. (ST. PAUL, MN; LLEWELLYN PUBLICATIONS, 1992). ISBN O-87542-018-4

BRYANT, PAGE. STARWALKING: SHAMANIC PRACTICES FOR TRAVELING INTO THE NIGHT SKY. (SANTA FE, NM: BEAR & COMPANY, INC., 1997). ISBN 1-879181-36-3

CAHILL, SUSAN, ED. WISE WOMEN: OVER 2000 YEARS OF SPIRITUAL WRITING BY WOMEN. (N.Y., NY: W. W. NORTON & COMPANY, INC., 1996). ISBN O-393-03946-3

DAVIS, JOHN PATRICK. CHRYSALIS. (AUDENREED PRESS, P. O. BOX 1305, #103, BRUNSWICK, MAINE O4011. 207-833-5016. 1997). ISBN 1-879418-86-X. THIS BOOK IS A BEAUTIFUL "POEM" OF ONE PERSON'S JOURNEY FROM DIS-EASE TO HEALING AND WHOLENESS THROUGH REASSESSING AND INTEGRATING THE VARIOUS ASPECTS OF HIS LIFE: MIND, BODY, EMOTIONS AND SPIRIT.

HALIFAX, JOAN. THE FRUITFUL DARKNESS; RECONNECTING WITH THE BODY OF THE EARTH. (HARPER SAN FRANCISCO, 1994) ISBN O-06-250313-8

KELLY, PENNY. THE ELVES OF LILY HILL FARM: A PARTNER-SHIP WITH NATURE. (ST. PAUL, MN: LLEWELLYN PUBLICA-TIONS, 1997). ISBN 1-56718-382-4

KUSHI, MICHIO. OTHER DIMENSIONS: EXPLORING THE UN-EXPLAINED. (GARDEN CITY PARK, NY: AVERY PUBLISHING GROUP INC., 1992). ISBN O-89529-450-8

SCHIMMEL, SCHIM. DEAR CHILDREN OF THE EARTH: A LETTER FROM HOME. (NORTHWORD PRESS, INC., P. O. BOX 1360, MINOCQUA, WISCONSIN 54548, 1994). ISBN; 1-55971-225-2. THIS BOOK IS ONE OF THE MOST BEAUTIFUL I'VE EVER EXPERIENCED. IT IS FOR CHILDREN OF "ALL AGES".

RECOMMENDED LISTENING

THE MUSIC OF DENEAN, INCLUDING "THUNDER", 1994 (WITH HOWARD BAD HAND SPEAKING LAKOTA LYRICS WITH THE VOICE OF PURE LOVE); "THE WEAVING", 1993; AND "FIRE PRAYER", 1991. EVERY BLADE OF GRASS SWAYS IN HARMONY WITH HER LYRICS AND MUSIC.

INDEX OF SAYINGS

AZTEC CALENDAR STONE

NO MAN CAN REVEAL TO YOU AUGHT BUT THAT WHICH
ALREADY LIES HALF ASLEEP IN THE DAWNING OF YOUR
KNOWLEDGE. FOR THE VISION OF ONE MAN LENDS NOT
ITS WINGS TO ANOTHER MAN. AND EVEN AS EACH OF
YOU STANDS ALONE IN GOD'S KNOWLEDGE, SO MUST
EACH ONE OF YOU BE ALONE IN HIS KNOWLEDGE OF
GOD AND IN HIS UNDERSTANDING OF THE EARTH.
                                    - KAHLIL GIBRAN
                                        THE PROPHET

FOR ADDITIONAL COPIES OF THIS BOOK, PLEASE SEND A CHECK OR MONEY ORDER IN THE AMOUNT OF $17.00 ($14.00 + $3.00 S&H) TO:

SHARON PACIONE
LOTUS HOUSE
P. O. BOX 360421
STRONGSVILLE, OHIO 44136

440-237-5226 (VOICE MAIL)
440-237-2831 (FAX)

OHIO RESIDENTS ADD 7% SALES TAX IN CUYAHOGA COUNTY AND 5½% FOR THE REST OF THE STATE. (MAKE CHECK OR MONEY ORDER PAYABLE TO SHARON PACIONE).

FOREIGN ORDERS WELCOME. POSTAGE AND HANDLING WILL BE ADJUSTED ACCORDING TO LOCATION.

ONE MUST NOT MISTAKE MAJORITY FOR TRUTH.
- JEAN COCTEAU
FRENCH POET
1889-1963

THE ANIMALS HAVE TOLD ME,
"WE ARE WORRIED, MOTHER EARTH.
WE ARE AFRAID
BECAUSE OUR HOMES ARE BEING DESTROYED
BY PEOPLE WHO DON'T KNOW BETTER,
OR DON'T CARE.
THEY DON'T KNOW
THAT WE ARE THEIR SISTERS AND BROTHERS.
MOTHER EARTH,
THESE PEOPLE ARE CUTTING DOWN
YOUR FORESTS,
DUMPING GARBAGE IN YOUR OCEANS
AND RIVERS,
AND FILLING YOUR SKY WITH POLLUTION."

FROM: DEAR CHILDREN OF THE EARTH
(A LETTER FROM HOME)
BY: SCHIM SCHIMMEL

...'TIS A PITY
THAT YE STILL DON'T UNDERSTAND
THE NATURE OF BALANCE.

FROM: THE ELVES OF LILY HILL FARM
BY: PENNY KELLY

HEAVEN IS SPREAD ABOUT UPON THE EARTH BUT MEN
DO NOT SEE IT.
                    - THE GOSPEL ACCORDING TO THOMAS

AN ETHICAL UNIVERSE
CANNOT BE UNDERSTOOD
IF IT IS APPROACHED
UNETHICALLY.

PAGE BRYANT
STARWALKING